Oh, you're look
You must be curious. (
the world curiously, and ...
    it. All sorts of poems in various forms.
I like writing in form.

What do you think you might find in my book?
You might be surprised. Surprised is good. In
2018 I got surprised a lot and wrote a lot of
surprising rhymes. There's a surprising rhyme or
two from other years in my book as well.
I hope you like them.

'So what's in the book, then?'
Sonnets. Villanelles. Limericks and triplets. Free
verse. Triolets. Nature and politics. Religion.
Psychology. Sweet rhymes and silliness.
Rhymes in which I'm a bit of a bitch.
Self-indulgent pieces of prose.
Really rather serious things.
Nothing like love songs.
And Mischief.

What else? Oh yes...

'Why the swearing?'
Why not?
'Is it therapy?'
No.

Thank you so much for
your interest in my work

Gail Foster

Devizes, December 2018

Other works

A Sudden Poet

The Great Life and Other Stories

A Curious Poet

Takin' The Pith

Smoke and Roses

If Truth Be Told

ISBN: 9781791500412

Contents

Seventeen Syllables p93

Silliness p103

Sadness p135

Not Saying p153

The Gorsedd p169

Prose p189

MISCHIEVOUS SPRING

a book of verse

Gail Foster

for

my friends
my family
my muse

and the
people who
get me

thank you

Ceres

My name is Ceres, Goddess of the Corn
I stand above the Market Place and stare
With stony face, half dressed, and with a horn
Towards the North, the hill, the over there
I've lovely hair, but long the days have passed
When men admired the firmness of my rack
I'm old, and to be fair I can't be arsed
Once had one's day is never coming back
I've sewn my seed, been fertilised, and borne
My little birds and thrown them to the skies
Seen men come to the Market Cross to mourn
Seen marryings, and mayhem in The Vize
I'm old, but oh I see, from up on high
The secret things, the glory of the sky

VARIOUS
RHYMES

*

The Cynic Speaks of Love

The Cynic speaks of Love: What lie is this
But lust dressed up in silky swathes of lace
In pretty words, and promises of bliss
Come pouting in her petticoats, her face
All flushed with rouge and scarlet on a smile
With kohl around her cold come-hither eyes
Come lie with me, my love, a little while
She'll say, and pat the bed, and part her thighs
And flash her stocking tops gone all awry
And secret places oh so sweetly blessed
And you'll believe, the Cynic said, as I
Who once was by her magic so possessed
In Love, when she is nothing but a whore
That's forty quid, she said, and that's the door

Water; a Warrior's Triplet
~ *for Susan Lomas and Dru Marland*

Spring, beneath the alders tall
Catkins kiss the river's fall
Light as always conquers all

Summer, and the oak is king
Larks above the waters sing
All are one with everything

Autumn, sunset on the vine
Rosy swans on seas of wine
All of this is yours and mine

Winter, ice around the hill
Yews and elders standing still
Empty cups be cups to fill

frost on the roof tiles

five minutes ago
there was frost on the roof tiles
and now it is gone

falling from the shining eaves
night, and the shadows of sun

What's the Crack with Rugby?
~ for my Dad, and Ian Diddams

So what's the crack with rugby?
My father used to play
He'd come home with an injury
Every other day
My mother used to worry
He was quite deaf to her fears
Her futile protestations fell
On cauliflower ears
Oh so many broken bones
As trophies he would wear
Those would be the only times
I heard my mother swear
My father didn't drink much
He didn't do the pub
But he'd sink some with the other lads
Down the rugby club
He had a book of rugby songs
Some of them were crude
Dinah, Dinah show us yer leg
And other ones more rude
A weird way to learn about
Sex and funny stuff
Sex Ed in the seventies
Was really pretty rough
Now I watch a rugby game
And find the blokes quite hot
Got to love a massive thigh
And firmly muscled bott
Oh how they thunder up the pitch
And grunt and sweat and shout
Got to love testosterone
It's what it's all about
Never mind the odd shaped ball

8

Shape doesn't make me frown
It's how they chuck the thing that counts
And how they smack it down
The scrum's a thing to marvel at
A tad homo erotic
What if someone breaks their neck
Not sport for the neurotic
And then there's the line dancing
And shouting things in code
Like massive noisy warriors
With faces streaked with woad
Not partial to the gumshields
I suppose they save the grief
Of ruining a toothpaste smile
And choking on the teeth
The thing I don't quite understand
Is how they pass the ball
What's the crack with backwards?
I don't get that at all
I'm a girl who loves a tryer
It's hardly a perversion
It just don't get more exciting
Than a finely placed conversion
Snorting mist like horses
Hot blokes running free
Imagine the baths afterwards
Oh it's all too much for me...

I have memories of autumn
Fields all churned up with mud
My Dad and Son played rugby
There's some rugby in my blood
So, here's my final word on this
Rugby's hot, but makes me sad
For when I think of rugby
It reminds me of my Dad

9

Hazel Tree Sonnet

My wild subconscious mind has given me
(And I would seek to know what it intends)
In dream, the seeming of a hazel tree
Please talk to me of hazel trees, my friends
I keened for wisdom, and in answer got
To keep me from the dark, and poverty
An Ogham tree, a nutshell, wand, or what
Please talk, my friends, of hazel trees to me
I hear you say the truth is mine to find
Within myself, or high up on a hill
But dearest friends, if you be good and kind
Please talk to me of hazels, if you will
And I will listen, and make sense of it
Ye Gods, my friends! I have a sonnet writ!

The Poets of Yore

It would have been easier back in the day
Before all the words became taken as read
Still all of the clichés for love left to say
In books yet unwritten and verses unsaid
In the halcyon days, before thousands of men
Filled all of the couplets with ice and with fire
All saying the same and the same thing again
In millions of rhymes about night and desire
As many as stars. I would write about love
But little remains I can claim to be mine
'She sees in the circle at solstice, a dove'
'You can't put a dove at the end of a line
In a rhyme about love! Well not any more'
Bunch of smug bastards, the poets of yore

The Devil's In The Marketing

Psst wanna buy a pretty thing
The spiv hid in the shadows said
(The devil's in the marketing)
Psst wanna buy a pretty thing
The silver moon slid shivering
Along his shiv, Or this instead
Psst wanna buy a pretty thing
The spiv hid in the shadows said

Psst wanna buy a pretty thing
It love you long time that for sure
(The devil's in the marketing)
Psst wanna buy a pretty thing
The pimp said as a passing king
Threw thirty pennies on the floor
Psst wanna buy a pretty thing
It love you long time that for sure

Psst wanna buy a pretty thing
The artist and the writer sighed
(The devil's in the marketing)
Psst wanna buy a pretty thing
A feather from an angel's wing
Fell fluttering, but no-one died
Psst wanna buy a pretty thing
The artist and the writer sighed

flaky

snow, or not to snow
make your mind up flaky sky
cat sniffs at the air

jumpy little birds
twitter on the frozen twigs
feathers, flurrying

coal in the wind, ice
crackles in the guttering
a cold slice of night

white smoke, winter cloud
threatening to overwhelm
all orion's stars

Orion; a sonnet

How cold you are, Orion, and how bright
Your belt of glittered stars, your hands and feet
As frost on stone, as diamonds in the night
As ice on glass, and statues in the street
I'm told you are a light from long ago
A huntsman froze before he made the kill
To rise in winter, rampant with his bow
To fall in spring, and die beneath the hill
How bold you are, and how you dominate
The sky between the Plough and Pleiades
The old canal, the bridge, the graveyard gate
The owls who haunt the shadows of the trees
Sing, Sirius, and all the stars divine!
How old you are, Orion, how you shine

Orion and The Moon; a villanelle

Come catch me then, Orion, if you can
We've played this game before. I play to win
I am the moon and you are just a man

The same old same old game since time began
We've started, so we'll finish. Let's begin
Come catch me then, Orion, if you can

Some lesser constellations also ran
I left them all stood standing in a spin
I am the moon and you are just a man

A man of stars, a huntsman, fiercer than
The lot of them, with finer light within
Come catch me then, Orion, if you can

Come chase me cross the spaces in the span
Before the night grows old and darkness thin
I am the moon and you are just a man

All stars must fall according to the plan
Before the morning I will have you sin
Come catch me then, Orion, if you can
I am the moon and you are just a man

Orion Is My Lover Now

Orion is my lover now
and will be till the winter's done
The fickle sun can take a bow
Orion is my lover now
and I his winter field to plough
I yield. The darkness has begun
Orion is my lover now
and will be till the winter's done

gossiping stars

last night
the stars said
after venus
went to bed
orion went
down on
the moon

scoring light

yesterday's sun, seen
pink striped and glory bright at
chippenham station

since then, no sightings, nothing
gone to bath to score some light

When I Was Small

When I was small I dreamed of tidal waves
and thought the spider's web above my bed
to be a disincarnate entity.
I learned to walk by falling down, and thought
that I was bigger than my body was
and wondered why the words I knew so well
refused to form, and why such things as mud
however long you watched them, didn't change.
I had the sense that hid behind a wall
were mysteries that once I understood.

I have no memories of former lives -
I only know that I was never young.

Gnid*

When I was young I read 'What Katy Did'
'Lolita', 'Heidi', 'Nineteen Eighty-Four'
The sexy books that my mate's mother hid
The 'Flower Fairies', 'Little Women', 'War
and Peace', (It bored me rigid, I confess
The Russians never were my cup of tea)
'A Clockwork Orange', and the Bible, bless
A plot that's wholly lost by Chapter Three
At nine, I read some Jung, a lot of Jong
A little 'Peter Rabbit', and 'The Rats'
A bit of Poe, and porn, which came along
Because I looked for it, I guess, and that's
The truth. I learned my secrets as a kid
From filthy books, and fairy tales, and Gnid

* see Enid Blyton's signature

High, High, High In The Tree

High, high, high in the tree
Kids who are so much
Cooler than me
Prettier, cleverer
Richer and fitter
I stand at the foot of the tree
Feeling bitter

High, high, high in the tree
Kids who are so much
Safer than me
Lions are coming
Weeping and beaten
I stand at the foot of the tree
Being eaten

The Hundred Metres Race

The hundred metres race at school
Was not much fun for girls like me
I wasn't fast, I felt a fool
The hundred metres race at school
I felt an arse, it wasn't cool
I finished last, they laughed at me
The hundred metres race at school
Was not much fun for girls like me

For some the hundred metres race
Was run already, and they won
The fit, the thin, the fair of face
For some the hundred metres race
Was fun, and was their happy place
Their shiny hair shone in the sun
For some the hundred metres race
Was run already, and they won

The hundred metres race. I see
The pretty girls all running fast
And coming first in front of me
The hundred metres race. I see
Embarrassment and jealousy
I don't run now. It's in the past
The hundred metres race. I see
The pretty girls all running fast

I Drank Because I Wanted To

I drank because I wanted to
until I knew I couldn't stop
It started with the one or two
I drank because I wanted to
the one or two and then a few
a few more and a few on top
I drank because I wanted to
until I knew I couldn't stop

I tried controlling how I drank
and couldn't. It was ever thus
The devil's bar is dark and dank
I tried controlling how I drank
the more I tried the more I sank
the more I stank of piss and pus
I tried controlling how I drank
and couldn't. It was ever thus

I drank because I wanted to -
the lies that spill out from our lips
The earth is full of dead men who
all drank because they wanted to
If you're like me it waits for you
a slow death of a thousand sips
I drank because I wanted to -
the lies that spill out from our lips

The Craic

Oh how I would frolic
Were I not an alcoholic
But I'll raise a glass symbolic
To the craic

Whisky makes me melancholic
And overtly diabolic
And it wouldn't be a dram, Sir
But a sack

The Question

A person asked me once why I was here
on earth that is, not standing at the bar
and waited for the answer to appear.
It's said that when you're ready teachers are
inclined to introductions, this one had
been watching from the wings a while to see
what things I did in public, and how bad
or indiscreet my private sins might be.
The music stopped. I looked him in the eye
and told him, being quite surprised to find
I knew the answer, and could tell him why
I find myself incarnate in this mind.
What's that you say? As if I'm telling you
You do your own work, I have mine to do.

Seven

Seven's a mystery
Superstition, some say -
Spirals and sequences
Secret imaginings
Silly old heresies.
Sssh. See, in the moonlight
Seventh waves, gathering.

the clock on the wall

the clock on the wall
tick tocking a life away
wishing for sunshine

one day there will be
silent clocks and nothingness
and no light at all

down in the green fields
hares' heartbeats are quickening
tick tock, tick tock, spring

The Moment

Beware the moment when the mind
Becomes aware that all is well
In which there is no fault to find
Nor worrying, nor woe to tell
'All happiness and all good things
Are here within the now and here!'
The fool from on the rooftop sings
As all the angels disappear
And demons gather on the hill
Attracted by his careless cry
To watch him fall, as fall he will
As all things fall that fly too high
And shine too bright and fly too fast
Enjoy the moment. See, it's passed.

Public Property

I'm living on the street, that does not make
Me yours to feed with food I do not eat
Though I may lay my hat before your feet
My history is not your tale to take.

I'm old, I'm poor, I'm ill, I haven't got
A pot to piss in, or a welcome mat
You still don't get to patronise, or pat
My head as if you think I've lost the plot.

I'm pregnant, I'm in prison, I'm alone
I'm lost, I'm frightened in a foreign land
I'm vulnerable, but not, you understand
Your bitch. My mind and body are my own.

So touch me not, nor tell my tale for me
For I am not your public property.

They Fought For You, Have You Forgot?

Shall I vote or not?
She died for you, have you forgot
Who fought for you so you can say
Shall I vote or not today?

Shall I vote or not?
She fought for you to have the choice
To use your vote, and use your voice
Or stay at home today

Shall I vote or not?
What sister are you who forgets
The suffering of suffragettes
So you can vote today?

Shall I vote or not?
They fought for you, do you forget
The women who don't have it yet
The vote, or yet a say?

Shall I vote or not?
What, woman, are you mad or what
They fought for you, have you forgot
The price they had to pay?

Shall I vote or not?
My sister, listen, hear the sound
Of hooves of thunder on the ground
Lest we forget the day

Shall I vote or not?
They fought for you, have you forgot
Who fought for you so you can say
Shall I vote or not today?

sunday

morning, come again
fat blackbird, sat on a fence
just can't be bothered

mist, the graveyard cat
contemplates schrodinger's doves
might kill 'em, might not

sunday - it's brilliant!
small birds flit from tree to tree
wild with excitement

The Revelation of God's Comic Timing

Ten old folk, one bloke and a priest, and me
on Sunday for the Book Of Common Prayer
Outside the church, electric swirls of air
excite the birds. Inside it's Trinity
The rain begins to fall. It's soft at first
the merest brush of rushes down the stone
around us. Then a flash of light, a burst
of thunder right above us, and the groan
of heaven, opening. So what, what's odd?
Good question. Not the storm, it went away
as quickly as it came. It's just that God
enjoys his little jokes, and that today
the reading was from Revelation Four
(verse five; the thunder) Comic timing. More.

Act One

The stage is set, and as the curtains rise
We see our hero hanging on the cross
'A triumph', and 'A rare treat for the eyes'
'A tale of passion, sacrifice, and loss'
The posters said, and all of the reviews
Spoke well of it; 'Superbly acted', 'Tight'
And matinees are free, so what's to lose
And we'll be cool at dinner parties, right?
We open popcorn. Then the lights go out
We wait a while in darkness, then the crash
Of cymbals from the pit, a woman's shout
A crown of thorns against the sky, a flash
And it is done. A few tears, then the queue
To get the beers in quick before Act Two

Act Two

The curtains rise. The stage is dimly lit
Cue morning in the garden, in the gloom
A woman weeps, two silent angels sit
Within the empty spaces of the tomb
Where once he lay, our hero from Act One
'My Lord is gone!' she cries, 'I know not where!'
Cue lights, cue shining spotlights like the sun
Cue shouting in the Gods, 'He's over there!'
'Behind you!' 'No he isn't!' 'Oh' she said
'I thought you were the gardener' He's not
He's got a crown of stars around his head
It's him! He's risen! Blimey, what a plot
It's done. Well, that was thirty quid well spent
We'll come again. I think that's what it meant

colours of sunday
~ for valerie, vince, and john

valerie and I
call the slice of chapel light
hockney and lemon

sunshine on silver
tails of little wriggling fish
feeding the thousands

vince by the fountain
twinkling as he talks about
beetroot and the times

gold on the mustard
seeds that grow in gospel leaves
scattered on the ground

black belt lay preacher
hurling holy water on
the red fires of hell

the peace, fingers crossed
wishing my heart was as white
as the altar cloth

shades of pigeon grey
orange plastic shopping bags
taking sunday home

devil's music

after church I play
devil's music, turned up loud
dance, ye angels, dance

angels dance like this
feathers flying, halos slipped
barefoot on the clouds

hedges

hawthorn, cow parsley
seething sweetly in the hedge
the white froth of may -
soft, scented with butterflies
luminous as a moon rise

The Festival Is Coming
~ for the Devizes Arts Festival

The Festival is coming
And it's going to be a blast
It's nearly June
It's coming
Hard and fast

Ann Widdecombe is coming
There. I've said it and I'm done
Oh and Toyah's
Also coming
Oh what fun

The Festival is coming
Blow the trumpets! Bang the gong!
Everybody's
Coming
Come along

Rain Dance

Waiting for thunder, waiting for rain
Waiting for lightning to strike on the plain

When will it come, when will it come
The heat of the sun on the skin of a drum

Watching horizons, watching the hills
Watching the widening cracks in the rills

When will it come, when will it come
One drop of rain on the skin of a drum

Dreaming of rivers, dreaming of seas
Dreaming of streams and delirious trees

When will it come, when will it come
Two drops of rain on the skin of a drum

Thinking of doomsday, thinking of drought
Thinking of reservoirs all drying out

When will it come, when will it come
Three drops of rain on the skin of a drum

Dying for water, dying of thirst
Dying of waiting for heaven to burst

When will it come, when will it come
Four drops of rain on the skin of a drum

Crying for mercy, crying for men
Cry for the rain to come falling again

Hearing it come, hearing it come
The beat of the rain on the skin of a drum

Waiting for thunder, waiting for rain
Waiting for lightning to strike on the plain

bus ride

shadows of oak trees
lying lazy on the fields -
the bus trundles on

rows of green roses
cockle pickers, cabbages -
bromham, flowering

sheep on the hillside -
over the horizon rise
black birds of morning

tor

sunrise in the east
flying high towards the tor
an arrow of geese

sunset on the sheep
a twinkling of twilight stars
night, blackberry deep

It's An Autumn Thing

It's raining and it's wet and grey
and chilly - it's an autumn thing
it happens every year they say
it rains, and it gets wet and grey
then all downhill to solstice day
the still, the rising of the spring -
It's raining, and it's wet and grey
and chilly. It's an autumn thing

The Smiling Sidesman

Do come on in, the sidesman said
And see the little Christmas trees
His smile was wider than his head
Come in, he said, and see them, please

I heard the bells, I said, and saw
The lights within the window bright
He smiled again, and closed the door
Behind me on the chilly night

The air rang fragrant with the smells
Of frankincense, and all things good
Of forest floors, and snowy fells
And cinnamon, and Christmas pud

And oh, the trees, each little tree
Much prettier than all the rest
Bedecked with love and charity
By busy bees who did their best

I found the one I liked the most
Beside the aumbry in the wall
The place they keep the holy host
For when the vicar goes to call

It's hard to say quite what it was
That drew me to that little tree
It wasn't like the rest because
It wasn't very glittery

It simply was, and simply stood
A humble home to paper birds
With just a little cross of wood
On top, and on the paper, words >

Like 'Joyfulness', and 'Welcoming'
And 'Praise', and 'Inclusivity'
The words of hymns that choirs sing
And prayers for the Community

Sweet scraps of scripture, psalm and song
Commandments, proverbs, testament
With 'Holy God, Holy and Strong'
And other words from heaven sent

'Be still, and know that I am God'
The letters writ in ancient hand
In fountain pen, by 'Nature', 'Yod'
And 'England's Green and Pleasant Land'

And then, the 'Love Your Neighbour' thing
So bright that it stuck out a mile
And 'Justice' and 'Respect', an' ting
In red gel ink, graffiti style

It really was a lovely tree
'St. John's' it said, upon the wall
For all its stark simplicity
It seemed to me to say it all

I like your tree the best, said I
The sidesman gave a little wink
Have you got something in your eye
Not I, he said, but you, I think

I'm not saying you lie, my dear
But this I know and tell you true
We didn't do a tree this year
Too many other things to do

I wasn't having that at all
I took the sidesman by the hand
And showed him...nothing...by the wall
I'm sorry, I don't understand

It seems you've seen our mystery
He smiled again, as was his way
You're not the first to see that tree
Nor will you be the last today

With that he showed me to the door
And wished me well, and said goodnight
And then I turned to wave, and saw
His halo twinkle in the light

Two Sonnets for Bridge 140

I'm here again, up on the bridge, the one
Beside The Wharf, and cemetery gate
I come to watch the rising of the sun
Upon the water, and at noon, of late
To spot the river rat and dodge the cars
And even later, when the town's asleep
To stop to hear the owl, and see the stars
And cold Orion shimmer on the deep
I'm always here. It's odd, but even when
I'm elsewhere, I can close my eyes and see
The ways the seasons turn, and turn again
The ways of waves, and ravens in the tree
And me, above the water, as a ghost
Returned to haunt the place I love the most

This bridge. I blush, for long ago I had
A lover, and I kissed him here. And here
He wasn't mine to kiss, but I was bad
And it was Spring, and he was hot, and beer
Had made me wanton, as it always did
But he was most enamoured by the drink
I blush, as I remember how we hid
Beneath the arch, and teetered on the brink
For almost half an hour. It wasn't good
Well, I was. He was rubbish, to be fair
I waited for the owl call from the wood
Nope. Nothing. I gave up and left him there
This bridge. I stop and blush, as I recall
The times I've come, and haven't come at all

GOOD 'UNS
BAD 'UNS

*

Angels

Some angels come in human guise
And I have met one on the street
An ancient one with burning eyes
Some angels come in human guise
With hidden wings to make us wise
He told me things and it was sweet
Some angels come in human guise
And I have met one on the street

A Birthday Rhyme for Chelsa Broom

Chelsa, you're feisty as fuck
I chuck you a bucket of luck
Birthdays are so
Passé don't you know
But Yo. Oh and PS they suck

Chelsa, I wish you a day
Of moderate mirth and wa-hey
Birthdays are Meh
But what do we care
We'll all soon be dead anyway

Chelsa, like seriously
I wish you all good things for tea
Be happy as well
And stuff. Fucking hell
That's quite enough bullshit from me

A Grampy from Grimsby called Mick
~ for Mike Hopkinson

A Grampy from Grimsby called Mick
Said 'Oi, my guitar playing's slick'
Then he fell off his chair
With his arse in the air
And by fuck did we give him some stick

Baby Jacob's Head

Come here, Baby Jacob
Baby Jacob's nanny said
Sit between these bookends
And I'll strap them to your head
It's a bold look, but distinctive
And quite flattering at that
Normal from the side but
From the front a little flat
And pointy. Really pointy.
Like a bag of pointy things
A massive bag of ancient and
Anointed pointy kings
Baby Jacob sighed a bit
His tea was going cold
And spat his silver dummy out
And did as he was told

Brexit Backstab Bitchfest

There once was a government who
Were divided and hadn't a clue
How to manage the exit
From Europe and Brexit
You first. Oh no, after you.

There once was a government who
Were at war. It was blue upon blue
As they edged down the halls
With their backs to the walls
You first. Oh no, after you.

There once was a government who
Were divided and nobody knew
What to do, so they bitched
And they backstabbed and stitched
Up each other. You first. After you.

Button Wars

Little Trumpy stomped his foot
'Look what Sloppy Steve has put!'
He said, and spitting out a sweet
Went red, and did another tweet

Little Trumpy's button glowed
As from his tiny fingers flowed
Such foolish words as children sing
In playgrounds when they're bullying

Little Trumpy, he's the boy
Just William crossed with Fauntleroy
And Violet, the spoilt chick
Who thcreamed and thcreamed till she was thick

And Little Kim. What can I say
Like who'd want him to come to play
Imagine games of pass the parcel
'OK Kim, you win' (you arsehole)

God save us from these little boys!
Their tantrums, and exploding toys!
'Say, my Dad's bigger than your Dad'
'My button's bigger, and it's rad'

Call the Nanny! Raise a shout!
Is Poppins anywhere about?
Or anyone who, without fear
Can clip the fat boys round the ear?

Tell them that it isn't clever!
Send them to their beds, whatever
Or maybe make a little chart
To stick gold stars on when they fart

Adults are in classrooms taught
That wars are in theatres fought
And not by little kids at play
Who trash the nursery each day

I do despair. Damn, what's to do
They've barely learned to hold their poo
But wait for one to chuck his ball
Out of his pram, and fuck us all

Chris's Amazing Technicolour Curtain
~ for Chris Greenwood

I closed my eyes
Was quite uncertain
Quite what the curtain
Was supposed to do

I'd heard that Chris
Had played a blinder
And made a winder
And some pulleys too

He'd made a beast
Of pink perfection
A theatrical erection
Quite a stunt to view

Up in the Gods
Stuff started scrolling
Round wheels a-rolling
As designed to do

A well oiled hum!
An upward flight!
The curtain zinged right out of sight
The ruching tucked up all quite tidy
I was left alone

Ah...

Crap Spies

There once was a couple of spies
Who were crap and who couldn't tell lies
And even the hit was
A little bit shit -
'It's the snow you know, gets in your eyes'

Said the spies 'We came over to see
The great spire of Salisbury
But it snowed and was icy
The pavements were dicey
And flights back to Russia were free'

There once was a couple of spies
Who were famous and couldn't tell lies
Whoever's recruiting
For Putin needs shooting
'We shot him already - surprise!'

Dale

When you're at the checkout counter
And you hear the beep
It won't be Dale having fun
On Supermarket Sweep

Dale's with the angels now
I hope they like his style
And let him have a trolley
And go wild in the aisle

Damian Green

So farewell then, Damian Green
You seemed rather polite and quite clean
And upright as well
But you never can tell
By the look of them quite where they've been

diamond studded doilies

days of dirty laundry
d-list celebrities
diamond studded doilies
and a dress

Done

Farewell, my false and fickle friend
You flattered me beyond belief
With songs and gifts, but in the end
You gave me only pain and grief
It seems I didn't play the game
According to the rules you set
Just like before, again, the same
How slow the heart is to forget
I've seen your colours fly before
Bright yellow, shining on the mast
What silly fool would so ignore
The red flag of the recent past
I guess that's me. Well, lesson learned
Fuck you and your twisty fun
I flick the Vs with fingers burned
We're done.

Easter Sunday
~ for John (Ted) Dexter

no cars on the road
all of the town sofa bound
food lulled and sleeping

walking home, a man
evensong's slow gentle peace
on him like monks' robes

old man and poet
meet in quiet communion
by the graveyard gate

souls of the same shade
in unspoken fellowship
watching the birds fly

on the bridge, silence
white blossom, silver water
Easter Sunday light

Farewell, Billy Graham

Farewell, Billy Graham
You went on and on and on
Jesus this and Jesus that
It's quieter now you've gone
But noisier in heaven
Can you hear the angels cry
Where's the fucking ear plugs, Billy?
Bye

Farewell Dennis Norden, Then

Farewell, Dennis Norden, then
For he, like other funny men
Was alright on the night before
But now he isn't any more

Fuck Off Elton

Elton John, Elton John
Says he's going. Isn't gone
And isn't going with some style
And won't be gone for quite a while

Elton John, Elton John
Is he going? Has he gone?
And if he hasn't gone yet, why?
Fuck off, Elton. Go on. Try.

Gavin Williamson

Gavin, my boy, have Defence
You won't have to make any sense
Just show them your smile
And they'll all run a mile
Which will save us some shillings and pence

The Gardener
~ for Colin Hopgood's family

The gates opened soundlessly.
You've come, said The Light.
I've brought you vegetables and flowers, said The
Gardener.
Hyacinths and cabbages and carrots and
marigolds.
They're beautiful, said The Light. Thank you.
No, thank you, said The Gardener.

Gareth Southgate

I remember nineteen ninety six
like it was yesterday - the penalty
the way that Gareth kicked the ball and missed
I bet he never thought that day that he
would ever be back in the game again
his name engraved in Lions' hearts, their
lips aflame with songs of praise, and men
in waistcoat shops, and women swooning where
he might have been. You've got to love a man
who wears his pride so modestly, who's cute
who wears a new suit stylishly, who can
(if dream we dare) bring home the Cup to boot
If on that fateful day he'd walked away
we wouldn't be here, would we. Let us play.

Genius

A man in a Writers' Group said
I'm a genius, look at my head!
It's so big and so wide
That it won't fit inside
So I have to live outside instead!

God Bless Them All (You First)

God bless the Inquisition for
When all is dead and done
Just another bunch of
Perverts having fun

God bless all the Nazis and
The paedos and the rest
Just misguided and to be
Forever blessed

God bless Saudi princes, it's
Not easy being royal
(Just a little bit of blood
And lots of oil)

God bless them all, forgive them for
They know not what they do
You first at the altar
After you

Holiday Sonnets

I understood he wasn't God, the day
He took me in a dinghy out to sea
And, as the paddle floated far away
Upon the Scottish wave, it came to me
This time he's got it wrong. We didn't die
And only I would call it touch and go
But I was small, and oh the waves were high
And oh the wind, the wild pull of the flow
The day he got it wrong. On other days
He got it right. When I was small my Dad
Would take us walking on the ancient ways
And climbing up the mountains. My Dad had
An outdoor light about him. My Dad gave
Me this one. 'Only cowards can be brave.'

I knew my boyfriend wouldn't do, the day
He took me walking on the eggshell sand
In Newquay, and I tripped, and fell and, hey
He laughed at me, and didn't take my hand
The day was hot, the sea and sky were blue
My ankle hurt like 'What the fuck?' (a sprain)
'Bad luck' he said, 'next time if I were you
I'd look where I was going. Use my brain
That sort of thing.' I'd got it wrong before
But not like this. His eyes were icy black
And glittering. He laughed a little more
And did a little twirl, and turned his back
A psychopath. They're so misunderstood
He did take me to Rosslyn. That was good.

Jacob's Tone

Jacob Rees-Mogg, Jacob Rees-Mogg
looks down his nose like he's sniffing a dog
or tossing a ball, or a scrap or a bone
to us all. I don't like him
I don't like his tone

Jeremy Corbyn, Let's Call Him

Jeremy Corbyn, let's call him
A Russian, a traitor, a spy
Dress him in red
With a cat on his head
And wait for the rumours to fly

Jeremy Corbyn, let's say he's
Hitler in curious guise
Paint him with blood
And then pelt him with mud
And see if it sticks as it dries

Jeremy Corbyn, let's call him
What shall we call him today?
Make him the king
Of a paedophile ring
And a lover of Anton LaVey

Jeremy Corbyn, let's say he's
A demon, a liar, a freak
The sum of our fears
And there's other ideas
But you'll just have to wait
Till next week

judas in the potter's field

there he is again
judas in the potter's field
tears beneath the tree

Kavanaugh

I think I got away with it
He said and raised his shaky hand
To swear an oath to stand and sit
In judgement over all the land

I think I got away with it
He wrinkled up his nose and swore
Upon the Bible. Holy writ
The Songs of Solomon and more

I think I got away with it
His lip twitched as he made his vow
The ladies did protest a bit
But bitches, who's the Daddy now

Lucy and The Birds

Last year, in summertime, a flock of birds
flew into church to search for food and shade
sang hymns with us, and listened to our words
and watched us from the rafters as we prayed
And every now and then, a bird would fly
the long path of the nave from west to east
and back, in search of some small piece of sky
or sacred crumbs left over from the feast
We opened all the doors where they flew in
and scattered seed upon the holy ground
but as the days flew by their cries grew thin
and soft hearts wept for sorrow at the sound
till Lucy, at the West Door, knelt to pray
and lo, they saw the light, and flew away

Mozart

Mozart wrote an opera
His opera was clever
But he never wrote another one
Not ever

Our Jerusalem
- on Donald Trump's visit to the United Kingdom

And in the heat of summer time
Walking by England's fountains seen
A man who thought he was a God
And King of England's pastures green

We did not countenance his crime
Drew lines upon our crowded hills
And sang Jerusalem, Trump is here
Among us - dark Satanic chills

Bring me balloons of tan and gold
Bring me cartoons and bold satire
Bring tea and beer; Oh, clowns untold!
Bring me the jokes that will not tire

I will bring cheese to fuel the fight
Or something silly in my hand
This isn't Trump's Jerusalem
And we don't want him in our land

Peter Stringfellow at the Pearly Gates

You're not coming in in a thong
Said Peter to Peter. It's wrong
On the angels it's hot
But on you mate it's not
And you're not on the list. Run along.

Ron

A wealthy old miser called Ron
Saved the heating for when he was gone
He froze, it was said
In a four-poster bed
With forty-three cardigans on

Stephen Hawking's Brain

It's not a bird, it's not a plane
It must be Stephen Hawking's brain
It's big enough, it's bold, it's bright
It's hurtling across the night
Towards an enigmatic hole
It's Stephen Hawking! Bless his soul

The things that Stephen Hawking said
Went flying right above my head
The physics stuff, the quantum quips
Equations, tricky little slips
Of space and mass and gravity -
All mystery and math to me

And me and Hawking disagreed
'The Bang!' he said, I said 'The Seed!'
And 'God knows why or where or what!'
But he could prove stuff I could not
So, hat doffed to a geezer who
Knew more than just a thing or two

It's Stephen Hawking! In the sky!
We watch his brain go flying by
A shining star! A scientist!
A twinkle-eyed ventriloquist!
And gone. Into a massive hole
Stephen Hawking. Rest his soul

the boy at the bus stop

the boy at the bus stop has
headphones and shades on
the boy at the bus stop has
serious grooves
the boy at the bus stop is
dancing away on
the pavement and busting some
serious moves
the boy at the bus stop has
downs and a song in
his heart and the beat of a
drum in his shoes

The Chuckle Brother

The auditorium is dim
The audience have flown
And he who once was you to me
Is him and he alone
To me, to...oh dear. Silence. Clap
The slap of stick on bone
The Chuckle Brother chuckles
On his own

The Morrissey Song

She stood on the corner, all wafty and wan
In tears, in a tee-shirt with Morrissey on
Her lover was lost and the last bus had gone

She stood on the corner, she tore out her hair
She looked up the road but no nothing was there
I told you, sang Morrissey, life isn't fair

She stood on the corner, she moaned and she
cried
As Morrissey groaned as if someone had died
In a song about crying but smiling inside

She stood on the corner, her heart fit to burst
He's lost and it's gone and I'm done for, she
cursed
The Morrissey song, though. That was the worst.

Toad

The greater spotted fat blond
Black suited backstabbing toad
Shits in his own pond and sings
Dreadful misogynist songs

Tommy Robinson

Poor little you, Tommy Robinson
Prison's not a place you'd like to go
Ho ho ho
You've got no keys, Tommy Robinson
Heaven's just a place for Christians, hey?
What's that you say?

We'd like to know a little bit about you on the
wing
We'd like to help you educate yourself
Look around you, all you see are empathetic eyes
Roll a cigarette up, feel at home

That's not your name, Tommy Robinson
You can bet we've got your number, though
Ho ho ho
We're fans you see, Tommy Robinson
Didn't you sing 'I'm Glad To Be Gay?
Back in the day

We'll take you to a secret place where no screw
ever goes
It's OK, Tommy, you can leave the cupcakes
It's just our little secret. We take all our mates in
there
Mostly though it's nearly always gobby racists
kids

You're slightly fucked, Tommy Robinson
Karma gets you in the end, you know
Ho ho ho
Hoo hoo get you, Tommy Robinson
Seems you've not got quite so much to say

Heh heh heh
Heh heh heh

Triolet
~ for Marcus Bales

I wrote a solstice triolet
It isn't good but it will do
It's not a form I've mastered yet
I wrote a solstice triolet
If Marcus can then you can bet
That I can fucking do one too
I wrote a solstice triolet
It isn't good but it will do

Tubby Bye Bye

Farewell, Tinky Winky
You were purple, with a red
Handbag in your tinky hands
And hanger on your head
And you taught a generation
To say 'Uh Oh' to the sky
Tubby Bye Bye Tinky
Tubby Bye

The Wiltshire Air Ambulance; a sonnet

What bird is this, I ask the man, that flies
The silken skies with shining knives for wings
We watch it slice the light above The Vize
And swoop and rise, and circle as it sings
Its melancholy song. I see him smile
A bird that beats the sparrows to the crack
Of dawn, he says. We stand a little while
I blink. It flies to Bristol, and flies back
He smiles again, and suddenly a tear
Appears to dance a trickle down his face
The bird has flown a sickly chick, my dear
To half a chance, and half a hope of grace
It flew me once. I look at him. Flew you?
Yes, me, he said. And someone else I knew

violin skies
~ in memory of leslie taylor

once within a time
particles arranged themselves
in common sense form

on blackboards, on hills
the questions of existence
written in chalk dust

antelopes, children
all wordsmiths and scientists
return to the stars

here was a good man
who showed in all his workings
the meaning of love

bring on the music
the flags and the festival
all the town rejoice

the physicist sits
and listens to the lark soar
in violin skies

I see him raise an eyebrow
to the mystery of life

SEVENTEEN
SYLLABLES

*

winter

the church clock has stopped
at two minutes past midnight
and still the birds sing

          winter, come as snow
          shivering on frosted twigs
          last year's baby birds

cassiopeia
flicks the vs at orion
and sirius winks

          eleven o'clock
          echoes from the battle fields
          men crying 'mother'

heathrow, eggshell sky
cracking open, broken by
the bright birds of planes

          marlborough high street
          waitrose, drizzled with raindrops
          landrovers, parking

white frost, half a moon
sunblushed in a winter sky
rose coloured seagulls

first light, sugar bright
frozen on the old canal
roses in the ice

> winter, the canal
> reflections of gulls hunting
> shadows in the ice

beyond the graveyard
somewhere in the quiet woods
snowdrops are singing

> here in the stillness
> in the poignance of silence
> the promise of light

two little brown birds
fluttered by the morning wind
dry leaves in a tree

> white sky, and pigeons
> dropping down the chimney pots
> snow, turning to rain

fingers crossed, fires lit
out there in the winter's night
woolly mammoths wait

spring

blue over arches
seagull shadows on the weir
bath in the sunlight

> bats, swallows of night
> shadows in the shallows swim
> fish ring, widening

suddenly, lifting
birds of the air in the bright
rain and the white sky

> clout cast, overcast
> over blown brown blossoms fall
> cat on pavement sat

crows' nest silhouettes
high above the river road
omens of summer

> one morning only
> shining in the window tree
> hosts of tiny stars

flowers, soft petals
the provocation of bees
stamens, quivering

sun, shining outside
inside silent curtains drawn
someone is dying

                    dark night, rustling trees
                    hid within the wind's rushes
                    helicopters, planes

bank holiday, rain
yesterday's chocolate stains
tantrums and telly

summer

wind in the maize field
green in the sun, fluttering
a mexican wave

                       summer, the sweet smell
                        of vomit and apricots
                          remains of the day

autumn

rain, running rings round
moorhens in the tree shadowed
khaki coloured deeps

november, dull skies
curtains open, curtains closed
no matter, no light

payday. tumbleweed
money in and money out
leaves, blown on the wind

autumn, home for tea
sirens in the wind, the leaves
falling on the hill

whatever

sunday night. nuff said
pack your dap bag up for school
baked beans, bath and bed

look, seven chinooks!
war is never beautiful
photographers weep

eight out of ten cats
are piss poor comedians
johnny vegas though

nineteen eighty four
in the ministry of love
the rats lie, waiting

haiku are like sheep
one haiku, two haiku; thought
ewe would like to know

underhand overs -
it's all over down under
weeping cricketers

night, and the spiders
underneath the furniture
blue light, flickering

~ for Brian Reid

sadness on the air
soft songs in the silent night
played on the heart's strings

SILLINESS

*

She Had Eaten Them All

'It's getting too hot in the kitchen', she cried
And turned off the cooker by tweaking a knob
And opened the window, and ran off outside
Leaving half of a bunny unboiled on the hob

As she walked in the garden she trod on a blob
Of frog. 'Don't you know' the frog said, 'I'm a Prince'
'Watch it' she said, 'I've a pot on the hob
And a hop out of turn and I'll turn you to mince'

The frog looked alarmed, and hid under a log
The bunnies had long gone, and all of the doves
Had flown, leaving only a dead horse to flog
By the stone where she buried the bones of her loves

'Oh, what did I say' she said, 'what did I do?
There's nobody nicer or sweeter than me!'
An owl raised an eyebrow. 'The problem is you
See them all as your breakfast, or dinner, or tea'

She thought for a while. She had eaten them all
And the garden, so empty, and eerie, and quiet
The hunger pangs, though, and the door in the wall...
Tomorrow, a more vegetarian diet

Otter

If you had to come to earth again, and choose
another form
And it had to be in winter, when it wasn't very
warm
Well you wouldn't be a seagull, for the sky is cold
as ice
And being something fishy in a pond would not be
nice
And you wouldn't be a starling, startled by a fall of
snow
Or something standing in a field with nowhere
else to go
No, you'd want to be much furrier, and have a lot
of fun
Who wants to be a little otter? I, for one.

Thoughts on 'Blue Planet II'

'The sea!' she cried
'Well' he said, 'what of it?'
'Why is there' she said
'Such a lot of it?'
'Somewhere, you know
For the fishes to go
And to throw all our shit
To get shot of it'

The Maintenance Man Meets Christopher Biggins

The maintenance man from Glasgow
Knocked on the door with his tool
Knock, knock, oh fuck me it's Biggins
One prefers to avoid as a rule
And he's scantily dressed in a bathrobe
That barely covers his bum...
This way, said Christopher Biggins
I've been eager for you to come

He took him along to the bathroom
He danced all the way down the hall
The maintenance man was nervous
But each to their own an' all
Here's my issue, said Christopher Biggins
The crack in the window pane
In need of a jolly good seeing to
As we all are now and again

The maintenance man got his tool out
Biggins looked rather impressed
I'm a fool for a tool he simpered
And some are more blessed than the rest
Then he posed, then he pouted a little
Then off he flounced down the hall
The window glass reflecting his arse
And the possible flash of a ball

The maintenance man had finished
He was good at a swift in and out
And Biggins was really unnerving
Like, what was the bathrobe about
I'm off, he shouted down the hall
I've sorted the window pane
Oooh, that was a quick one, said Biggins
Come again

I Married Him Forever

I married him a month ago
My only love and true
Cue hearts and flowers
And angels and
A teddy bear or two
And matching towels
And toasters and
Confetti from above
I married him forever and
I married him for love

I married him a month ago
I knew he was the one
Cue souls entwined
In harmony
And endless bedroom fun
And breakfast on the
Terrace with
A rose upon my plate
Our love will last forever and
My soul has found its mate

I married him a month ago
But then disaster struck
Cue man with sticky willy
When we hadn't
Had a fuck
Cue ringing up the telly
And then taking him on Kyle
I married him forever
For a while

Pickled Onion Monster Munch

Pickled Onion Monster Munch
The tickled tongue, the guilty crunch
The crumby lips, the fickle kick
The purple bag, the mini-sick
The stink of onions, hint of sin
And crumpled packet in the bin
The monster grins. You belch a bit
You wish you'd eaten healthy shit
But hey, they hit that pickle spot!
You smell of onions. Quite a lot

Andy Said
~ for Andy Fawthrop

'Oh, the rain! The cold! The pain!
My soul is old and dead!'
'Get over yourself, for fuck's sake'
My mate Andy Fawthrop said

'But oh, the winter, and the dark!
My heart! My mental health!'
Andy quaffs another beer
'For fuck's sake get over yourself!'

'But Andy! Don't you understand
The poignance of my pain?'
Andy sighs, and rolls his eyes
And says the same again

'But Andy..!' 'Bollocks!' Andy thought
'This bullshit breaks my brain!'
'Fuck off, and when you've got over yerself
Get over yerself again!'

'But oh the rain! The cold! The pain!
My heart! The winter! Night!
And all the mean things Andy said!'
The fucker. But he's right.

Granny's Pudding; a Moral Tale

'What shall we do with the bread?
We've got eighty two loaves in the shed
And we've spent all our money
On milk that smells funny
And raisins, stashed under the bed!'

'We shall make a gurt pudding!' said Gran
As she rolled up her sleeves and began
To knead as she muttered
'Tossers', and buttered
A cake tin the size of a van

'Gran, the AGA's a bit overloaded!'
'You what dear?' 'Oh no! It's exploded!
And the kitchen's all splattered
With bread pudding batter
Making more of a mess than the snow did!'

'That'll show you!' said Gran (she was wise)
Oh, the mischievous glint in her eyes!
'That the road of excess
Leads to mayhem and mess
Now I'm off down the pub for some pies.'

Plumber

I'm a poet
What a bummer
Far too late to
Be a plumber
A fucking poet
Writing tosh
For fuck all fame
And fuck all dosh
But for the fucking
Sake of...what?
Who'd be a poet
I would
Not

Be a poet!
Who said that?
You did. I did?
What a twat
Am I that fucked?
Is it too late?
To learn to be
A plumber's mate?
Picks up plunger
Thinks a bit
Puts plunger down
And writes more
Shit

we got mopeds

we got mopeds
brum brum brum
we're as cool as
cool can come
hard boys, bad boys
tut tut tut
round the corner
put put put
up the speed and
feel the burn
oops
nearly lost it
on the turn
but no-one's looking
that's OK
we're young, we're free
we've got all day
and we got mopeds
brum brum brum
we're the cool kids
ask our mum

Leopard Print

Leopard print! Not up for that.
But life's a jungle! Life's a stage!
Bet Lynch in her coat and hat...
Just saying. No! It's all the rage!

Leopard print! Don't bother. Don't.
Just try it! You'll look really hot!
I won't you know, I really won't...
It suits you! Oh. Well maybe not.

Leopard print! Look, no. Just no.
But, skittish shoes with kitten heels!
And oh, a little pussy bow!
Cue itty bitty fashion feels...

Leopard print. Well maybe. No!
You're right. It's not the look for you!
But (purr) the handbags! Hairslides, though!
And furry thongs! In red! And blue!

Leopard print! Hey, Grr! Miaow!
I'm feline, feral, fresh and fun!
What the fuck? Oh sorry. Wow.
You're wearing it. What have I done?

It's leopard print! I got the look!
It's me! In Bet Lynch coat and hat!
Oh dear, I'm sorry, I mistook
You for a scabby tabby cat.

Knickers, or Not?

The sun is here, the sun is hot
The game is off, the game is on
It's hot in here and then it's not
Knickers off, or knickers on?

The sun is here, the sun is gone
It's cold in here and then it's hot
Now you see it, now it's gone
Knickers on, or knickers not?

The Sky Is Blue

'The sky is blue'
said the pigeon
'Coo'
And so it was
And off he flew

Pot Noodles and Shit

To eat the Pot Noodle or not
Is the question. It's cheap and it's hot
And that's about it
On Pot Noodles and shit -
Bits of sweetcorn that float in a pot

Pot Noodle! You don't do you? Yes
I live on the edge. Do you? Bless
Enjoying the sleaze
Of a Noodle with cheese
And the street cred, I have to confess

I've eaten it. Have you? For real?
Yeah, really. Hey, how do you feel?
A little unwell
There's a right funny smell
In the kitchen as well. What a meal.

Plop

A poet there was who could not
Write poems and therefore was not
A poet at all. But she
Pushed out a small
Limerick. Plop. In the pot.

Christmas Pigeon

I'm a Christmas pigeon
I'm really in a flap
There's nowhere in The Brittox
I can land to have a crap
And Santa's bloody reindeer
Are cluttering the sky
I'll give you ding dong merrily
Merrily on high

I'm a Christmas pigeon
I'm not feeling very jolly
I landed on a perch bedecked
With bits of feckin' holly
I'll give you ding dong merrily
From merrily on high
Here's some crap for Christmas
In your eye

No-one Fancies Santa

No-one fancies Santa
I reckon it's the beard
And the coming down the chimney
Which is weird

No-one fancies Santa
He's asexual and odd
And he comes just once a year
A bit like God

No-one fancies Santa
The beard gets in the way
And he comes with so much baggage
On his sleigh

No-one fancies Santa
He's unusual, you know
When he comes he kind of jingles
Ho ho ho

No-one fancies Santa
He isn't really hot
But you know he's coming anyway
Or not

Piped Music

Shopping in Tescos
And back down the Mall
Stocked up with baked beans and left with fuck all
Still with an awful lot more to acquire
As they carry their bags to
The Mull of Kintyre

Pity The Christmas Toilet

Boxing Day, before the dawn
The peace before the rush
How silently the toilets wait
For morning's fatal flush
Small moments of serenity
Before the storm descends
And all of Britain passes Christmas
Out their bottom ends

How silently, how stalwartly
The toilets wait in dread
For all the nations bums to drop
Their bombs from overhead
And suddenly they're on us!
Merry Christmas, chocs away!
Half a ton of shit per bum
And all that remains of the day

Boxing Day, and after dawn
Left blocking up the bog
Yesterday's festivities
And Granny's chocolate log

Voldemort

Begone, foul flu, return to whence you came
The bogs of hell, where streams of burning snot
Flow sluggishly through caverns dull with flame
And sickly winds blow hot and cold and hot
Begone, foul flu, and take your aches and pains
Your bag of shadows and your poisoned wine
Your dogs of darkness, all your demon strains
And slink away to where the sun don't shine
You've had your fun, like Voldemort at play
Made every kiss a curse, and breath a cough
You pissed on Christmas, and on New Year's Day
You've had your day. It's time that you fucked off.
The demon hissed a bit, and made a smell
And spat, and missed, and slunk back off to hell

A Fly From Devizes

A fly from Devizes, he flew
Ninety-nine hundred and two
Missions - a flutter
A crap on the butter
And off. What a hero. Who knew

I've Got Some Soap Already, Thank You Love

Lorraine is in my newsfeed
She is trying to sell me Dove
As if I haven't got some soap
Already, thank you love
It seems that Facebook thinks
Because I've seen her on the telly
She can sell me fucking soap
And that I'm smelly

You've got to love Lorraine
She's hale and wholesome, not like me
She's cute and clean and shiny
And has yoghourt for her tea
It seems that Facebook thinks
That she's the one to sell me Dove
I've got some soap already
Thank you, love

Lorraine again. I'm scrolling past
She really is persistent
Popping up to flog me soap
When news is non-existent
It seems that Facebook thinks
That our Lorraine's the one to sell
Me moisturising soap
And that I smell >

Thanks, Lorraine. I'm sure the Dove
Is lovely, and for you
It smooths the wrinkles out
As well as Photoshop can do
I've got some soap already, though
I don't know what it's called
But it doesn't fall to bits
And cost fuck all.

Conspiracy Theories

There once was a bloke who said that
The earth wasn't round it was flat
To gather his proof
He stood on the roof
He's at it again, they said. Twat

There once was a bloke who said he
Was Jesus and climbed up a tree
He'd preach on his creed
For a while then he'd
Come down when he wanted a wee

There once was a bloke who said things
About ruling reptilian kings
And the Queen, who he said
When her skin is all shed
Looks like Smeagal from Lord of the Rings

There once was a bloke who said they
Can hear every word that we say
And fashioned a hat
Out of tinfoil and sat
In a tent in his bedroom all day

There once was a bloke who said no
To science. It's bullshit you know
He'd say as he read
Nostradamus instead
And the Sun, for the horoscopes though

There once was a bloke who said we
Are controlled by Illuminati
If you think that sounds shit
Then you try putting it
In a limerick. Gold star for me

Ew

There once was a girl who said Ew
It looks like I just cooked a poo
But with onions and sauce
And some cheddar of course
And my eyes shut I think it will do

There Once Was A Town Where It Rained

There once was a town where it rained
On a Market Day. People complained
To the council, and went
On to Facebook to vent
It's the weather, somebody explained

There once was a town in the Shire
Where people seemed never to tire
Of moaning. The weather
The parking. Whatever
The dogs and the cyclists. Dire

There once was a town where the sun
Shone for forty-five minutes and done
'It's too hot!' they complained
Quite a lot. Then it rained
Which confused them a bit. Which was fun

The Curse of Strictly (Come Dancing)

The Curse of Strictly
What's the chance
Take two people
Who can dance
And dress them up
In not a lot...
Slow, slow, quick, quick, frot

The Curse of Strictly
No surprise
Take two people
And four thighs
And add some lights
To make it hot...
Slow, slow, quick, quick, frot

The Curse of Strictly
What a shock
Take two people
Tits and cock
You dancin'? What
Nice bits you've got...
Slow, slow, quick, quick, frot

SADNESS

*

stations

two in the morning
empty stations of the heart
and the last train gone
lonely ghosts and lovesick fools
whistle at the frozen moon

Berries

The berries in the hedge were red
And summer's dust was on the sloes
How soft she was, the old man said
To touch, her lips were berry red
How much I miss her in my bed
Her merriness, the scent of rose
The berries in the hedge were red
And summer's dust was on the sloes

grief

candles on the bridge
flicker in the falling light
flowers by the wall

nothing to see here
a boy alone and weeping
as the cars go by

My Love Lay On The Market Cross

My love lay on the Market Cross
His heart was beating slow
I covered him with both my wings
Oh how I loved him so
The sun came up the sun went down
I lay with him until
He sighed and said he loved me and
His beating heart was still

Poppy Wars

The dead don't care
what colour poppy
you wear -
if it's knitted
or a diamante stud
for dead men stare
with blinded eyes
and their despair
is the colour of
the khaki in the mud

The dead don't care
what colour poppy
you wear -
white for peace
or purple, red for blood
they gave their lives
so you could have one
their despair
is the colour of
the khaki in the mud

quiet as the grave

tonight in the neighbourhood
there were police cars
hours and hours of
coming and goings in
landrovers, vans and in
various vehicles
something to do with
blood and with
smashing things
people with gloves on
and everyone whispering
now it has all gone
quiet as the grave

Tod

My mother put me in my cot
I woke up middle-aged and odd
The bit between I have forgot
My mother put me in my cot
I dreamed a bit and cried a lot
I woke and I was on my tod
My mother put me in my cot
I woke up middle-aged and odd

Years of Hurt

Oh God, did England win? That means that he
is Coming Home. I've done the washing up
and cooked him steak and crinkle chips for tea
and put his tinnies and his football cup
beside his chair and switched the telly on
All done. I wait. It could go either way
Of late it's gone a little bit like this
He comes in in a 'you're alright mate' way
insisting on a bear hug and a kiss
and then the beer kicks in - his tea is cold
his boss is mean to him, his car is shit
and I'm the Germans, oh and I am old
I told the girls at work he didn't hit
me, lied about the bruise beneath my shirt
Don't talk to me of Lions. Years of Hurt.

Drunk, with Love

Today, in Bath, I saw a drunk
Embrace the world with open arms
He'll be, by when the sun has sunk
Not quite so eager for her charms
And there'll be anger, old regrets
And sorry tears for lovers lost
And in the morning, shakes and sweats
And reasons to count up the cost
But for a moment, can in hand
The world's an oyster full of pearl
More glorious than God had planned
His beautiful, belovéd girl

embers

cool, freezing even
embers fade in fireplaces
in the morning, ash

Feathers of Ghosts

White horses riding, high on the hill
Chalk on the paths and the luminous glow
Of feathers of ghosts falling
Soft through the still
And the snow

Oh Mother, Oh God

I read that a man
at the end of his days
cries for his mother
and God

We all say goodbye
in our different ways
(I remember I thought
it was odd)

I never believed
in a God anyways
and mother was fond of
the rod

But I think of her now
as I lie in the haze
and my blood seeps
deep in the sod

As I lie in the mud
in the sun's last rays
- though I never believed
I would cry out the phrase -
I am but a man
at the end of his days

I'm dying
Oh Mother
Oh God

the wind on the battlefield

they all went down
first one, then two
and the wind
on the battlefield
blew

they all went down
first one, then two
men of the town
that everyone
knew

they all went down
first one, then two
and the wind
on the battlefield
blew

They Never Went To War

They never went to war; they stayed at home
The young, the old, the unwell and the dead
The women who were not allowed to roam
The men who tilled the fields and baked the bread
Those sat in darkness waiting for the rap
Of letterbox, and soft white feather fall
The silence broken by a dripping tap
Dark shadows cast by street lamps on the wall

The little lads who ran behind the train
That took their fathers off to certain death
Who waved until their arms ached in the rain
Who ran until their lungs ran out of breath
Old men who yearned for youth; just one more chance
To feel the blood flow, hear the battle cry
To wear the uniform and take a stance
To stand with other men, to fight and die

The crippled and the mad, the deaf, the blind
Escaped the fate of many thousand men
Some angry that they had been left behind
Some thankful that they'd never fight again
The women who with sleeves rolled ploughed the land
Lit candles, raised the children, hid their tears
Made ammunitions with a careful hand
Kept watch and saved the night time for their fears

So many stayed at home, and stayed alive
And suffered pain and loss, regret and guilt
That they were left, that they were to survive
Within the house such sacrifice had built
Their many names are not inscribed on stone
Those sorrowed souls, so haunted by war's ghost
Were left to stand and mourn the dead alone
And listen to the trumpet sound the post

NOT
SAYING

*

Brief Encounter Triolet

You looked me in the eye, I knew
You would if given half a chance
I would have done and you would too
You looked me in the eye, I knew
You wanted me, I wanted you
We could have at a second glance
You looked me in the eye, I knew
You would have given half a chance

Over-Arting

I will paint you a picture of pleasure, she said
Depicting delight in delicious design
Is quite a particular passion of mine
I will paint it in blue with a mischievous red
And you will be led by an impudent line
Into shadows as deep as desire is divine
Or maybe the colours of roses instead
Be best to express this obsession of mine
'The last light of summer, catching the shine
On a dishevelled rose, on a dishevelled bed
Oh sweet inspiration, I drink of your wine!'
At that she tripped over the cat (it was fine)
It's your fault, she said, you just go to my head
Just give us a shout when yer finished, he said

wink

sometimes
I wink
at you
with my
mind's eye

Quite

Close the door quietly there as you go
So I don't hear you leaving, my never quite dear
But he never quite left, because really you know
He was never quite here

Needy Leaf

I'm loath to leave you, said the needy leaf
I've loved you since I was a little bud
Oh, leave it out, the tree said, stay your grief
You'll still be here, it's just that you'll be mud
She contemplated winter on her knees
Before his trunk - 'twas not that bad at all
He after all was King among the trees
So mote it be, the leaf said, let me fall

Twitter. Twitch. And Coo.

Horny owls to woo to wit
And randy pigeons coo
Me, I twitter like a tit
When I think of you

Mad dogs roll around in shit
And moony cows go moo
Me, I twitch my tail a bit
When I think of you

Dozy does do flirt and flit
And pussies purr and mew
Me, I think you're really fit
Twitter. Twitch. And coo.

Going

Are you going now, or gone
And should I cry, or should I wait
For when you shut the garden gate
And wave and walk into the sun?

Should it be then, or it be now
The long farewell, the last goodbye
The day you turn and take a bow
And leave me at the gate to cry?

I know it's coming anyway
The day when you and I are done
Let it be then and not today
I see you
Going
Going

Gone

Sapphics?

Sapphics; ancient, serious rhymes, no place for
Faint hearts, handbags, dancing like no-one's
watching
Losing my religion stuff. Corner. Hard core
Stripped down and naked

Old school, barefaced, knickerless rhymes, no
place to
Hide, half-hearted, dressed up in skirts for
Sundays
simpering in limericks; will you, won't you
Chase me and kiss me

Oh no. These are doves on the altar rhymes, for
Star crossed lovers, halcyon days, all or nothing
Days of hot blood, spilled from the veins, all raw,
and
Red in the sunlight

Here you go, then; Here on this altar, I slay
Doves for you, my only and most beloved, with
Breasts laid bare. Not loving the dead doves, you
say
Nice pair of tits, though

Flounce

'The time will come when I am over you
a few more moons, and later down the line
a few more rhymes, a bitter tear or two
some issues to work through, and I'll be fine
Though for a while there'll be an empty space
within my heart where once you used to be
there'll soon be someone else, another face
to take your place and play the muse for me
You know that, don't you? Anyway, fuck you!
We'll soon see who'll be leaving who behind!'
And off she flounced, as feisty lovers do
'No sooner out of sight than out of mind!
And if you think I'm waiting you're a fool!'
'I'll catch you later, then.' 'Yeah, maybe. Cool'

the earth and the rain
~ for you

the earth is hard and hot and dry
and waiting for the rain's wet kiss
to fall down from the treacle sky
the earth is hot and hard and dry
the air too thick for birds to fly
it's just a waiting game is this
the earth is hard and hot and dry
and waiting for the rain's wet kiss

the rain will come, you know it will
come falling soft and warm and wet
in rivers round the ancient hill
the rain will come, you know it will
and every niche and crack will fill
it's been so long that you forget
the rain will come, you know it will
come falling soft and warm and wet

you are my earth and I would kiss
you wet and sweetly like the rain
it's just a waiting game is this
you are my earth and I would kiss
you, be the sizzle and the hiss
of water on your burning plain
you are my earth and I would kiss
you wet and sweetly like the rain

Heartburn

You stir my heart a little bit
It might be indigestion though
I think you're funny and you're fit
You stir my heart a little bit
It's beating hard beneath my tit
I've eaten cheese but even so
You stir my heart a little bit
It might be indigestion though

Poster Boy

I like your photo. I might print it out
and stick it on the bit of wall beside
my Bieber poster. I think it's the eyes
I like the way they follow me about
I like that. I might go and print it out
In black and white, and in a bigger size
You'd like a nice matt finish I surmise
I'd like that too. I look at you, and pout
I'm pouting at your photograph. It's true
You're smouldering a little bit. It's hot
I like that subtle sideways thing you do
It's sexy and you know it, but you're not
As hot as Bieber. 'What?' I think A2
Will do it nicely, Poster Boy, don't you?

monday

standing room only
on the bus today -
in the space
inside myself
I find you and smile

Not Saying

I never said I loved you, that would be
the end of you and me, and be untrue
Not saying it to you, nor you to me
nor would we, even if we wanted to.
I never said I loved you, never said
that we should be together, or desired
to be the one and only in your bed
or been by lust or loneliness inspired
to own you. Oh, but how I miss you now
It isn't love, it's just a little pain
like heartburn, or like indigestion, ow
It hurts like fuck. Not saying it again
I never said I loved you, and I won't
be saying that I love you, and I don't.

THE
GORSEDD

*

Burning Angels; Winter Solstice 2017

So many kings of old have come to me
At midnight, in the winter, at the still
In crowns of holly, clothed with mystery
Come riding proudly down from yonder hill
With torches flaming, salamander eyes
Ablaze with ancient summers full of lust
And I have had them all between my thighs
And I have turned them all to ice and dust
Except for he who keeps my fires alight
When darkness falls too deep to understand
Who lies with me all winter, till the night
Recedes, and spring returns to seed the land
With him I make, beneath the mistletoe
The burning shapes of angels in the snow

Mark the Bard
~ for Mark Westmore

There once was a Druid called Mark
Who could slam about sun and the spark
Whilst not whiter than white
He was less of the night
And more of the day than the dark

A Bard from the Avebury hood
He would whittle his words from the wood
Add a berry of yew
And some mistletoe too
And bang in the net...he was good

My Goddess, that Druid could rap
In the spring he could draw up the sap
And in winter could beat
Up the heat through his feet
Pretty neat...give the Druid a clap

The Green Beneath The Snow

the hills are growing green beneath the snow
white horses, shake the winter from your manes
the spring has come, the wild wind told me so

cold ice be gone, and warm sweet water flow
come, crocuses, and flower on the plains
the hills are growing green beneath the snow

grey gulls fly high, and clouds of blossom blow
come, laughing crows, and dance within the rains
the spring has come, the wild wind told me so

soon summer, and so many seeds to sow
come, sun, spill down the furrows of the lanes
the hills are growing green beneath the snow

bright gorse ablaze, and alder tops aglow
come blood, and flood the burrows of the veins
the spring has come, the wild wind told me so

dark night be gone, long days of light to go
come love, with all your mysteries and pains
the hills are growing green beneath the snow
and spring has come, the wild wind told me so

Mischievous Spring

A mischievous season called Spring
Liked to tickle the tree tops an' ting
And teach songs to the birds
Full of old-fashioned words
Oh the rude songs Spring taught them to sing!

Spring liked to laugh, and to run
On the hill tops and wind up the sun
With a glint in her eye
And the hint of a thigh
And her hair down and buttons undone

Sometimes she'd knock off a joke
How the squirrels would squeak as she spoke
And oh how the tits
Loved the sniggery bits
Of the ones for the feistier folk!

Spring liked the tease and the chase
Oh the flirtatious look on her face!
Catch me! She'd say
Always getting away
Well, not always. A time, and a place

A word, Winter said, in your ear
You're crossing a line here, I fear
Enough of the bants
And the flashing of pants
It's most unbecoming, my dear

Winter, said Spring, you're as old
And as wet and as grey and as cold
As a sheep in the mud
While I've fire in my blood
I shall not do a thing that I'm told!

And off she went, flicking the Vs
I am Spring, and I'll do what I please!
Off to dance in the ring
With no knickers an' ting
And to tickle the leaves in the trees

Me Name Is May
~ for Terry Dobney

Me name is May,
Me skirts are full of blossom, don't you know
And in me eyes are twinklings of flame
I have to say
I court the wind, and when the breezes blow
I scatter all me petals, that's me game

I'm flirty as
And I make Spring look like a timid nun
That knicker thing a silly little trick
I have to say
That if you like it wilder I'm the one
For lightin' fires, and ticklin' a wick

Me name is May
I'd like to wind me willow round yer pole
Why, thank you Sir, I don't mind if I do
I have to say
I know a secret place to have a roll
Feel free to bring yer pole along with you

I'm flirty as
The wind that whips the blossom from the trees
As fresh as flowers, innit, I got class
I have to say
There's things that I won't do, for all the tease
Oi! Who said you could poke me in the grass?

Me name is May
And you may dance with me upon the hills
Good Sir, that's if you've got the energy
I have to say
I'm really only in it for the thrills
And I'll be gone tomorrer, wait and see

I'm flirty as
You're feelin' it - that sudden gust
That comes all unexpected from behind
I have to say
I'm all for spontaneity and lust
But really, leave it out, mate, do you mind?

Me name is May
Or maybe not. I see that you're still
Burning with desire
I have to say
The flames were hot but just a little practice will
Enable you to leap a little higher

Me name is May
Oh are you done, you've sewed yer seed
Already, bless yer soul
I have to say
That it was fun, a little quick perhaps but
Hey, God speed, Good Sir, and
Don't forget yer pole!

The Blossom On The Bough

The fires are lit, my lover, and the hills
are flickering with little points of light
The sun is set, and deep within the rills
the seeds of stars are littering the night
The smoke is rising, lover, rising high
in winding spires of ribbons in the air
and in the rivers where the willows cry
and on the leys the ancient druids dare
to walk, the chalk is glowing. I know you
will never leap the Beltane fires with me
or rise on one May morning in the dew
beside me, spellbound by my poetry
Or so it seems. But oh, my lover, how
the blossom burns, so brightly on the bough

The maypole's up, my lover, on the green
its willow ribbons flutter in the breeze
I would you be my king, and I your queen
for one night only, here beneath the trees
The hawthorn froths, my lover, in the hedge
the buds are bursting, birds are nesting high
yet still you fly, my hawk, above the edge
of some cold mountain way up in the sky
Come down, or are you wary that a flame
might fall within your feathers, or a spark
ignite your heart, or god forbid, you came
to want to stay beside me in the dark
It's so, it seems. But see, my lover, now
the blossom burning brighter on the bough

Solstice Triolets

The height of summer, and the light
High fiving round and round the ring
The fireflies are burning bright
The height of summer, and the light
Gone glimmering on birds in flight
And in the stones a shimmering
The height of summer, and the light
High fiving round and round the ring

The heat of summer, and the scent
Of roses hanging in the air
The skylarks sing in wild ascent
The heat of summer, and the scent
Of oak smoke rising heaven bent
The laughter ringing from the fair
The heat of summer, and the scent
Of roses hanging in the air

The light of summer, and the beat
Of drummers, and the humming bees
The blood of life runs hot and sweet
The light of summer, and the beat
Of thunder, and of dancing feet
The lightening striking in the trees
The light of summer, and the beat
Of drummers, and the humming bees

The Song of the Wren

The wren is singing, high up in the tree
Come, lay your crown beside me on the ground
Come lie with me, my love, come lie with me

For every bloom on earth there is a bee
For every queen a green king to be crowned
The wren is singing high up in the tree

I wore a gown of bright embroidery
I wear my hair with heather flowers wound
Come lie with me, my love, come lie with me

I'm wanton, wild, alive with energy
I want you brought to me in oak leaves bound
The wren is singing high up in the tree

Oh aye, what then, why then I set you free
Oh my, and we get dirty and profound
Come lie with me, my love, come lie with me

You are my king. I shut my eyes and see
Your silhouette, with sunlight all around
I hear the wren sing, high up in the tree
Come lie with me, my love, come lie with me

Frack Song   ~
to be sung to the tune of
'Mud, Mud, Glorious Mud'

Frack, frack, let's have a frack!
It's all about money, we all know the crack
Shoot shit down a hollow
Fuck knows what will follow
Not easy to swallow, but let's have a frack

Streams, streams, what of the streams?
What of the water that runs through the seams
Polluted, permuted
Re-routed...Disputed?
So show us the science then - what about streams

Quakes, quakes, earth shakes and quakes
Ask them in Blackpool who wobbled their Flakes
Is wasn't Godzilla
Cruella? Cuadrilla
The Cavalier Driller - so what about quakes

Cost, cost, what about cost?
Too late to reclaim the land that is lost
Once it is shattered
And riddled and battered
You'll all say it mattered and count up the cost

Sense, sense, it doesn't make sense
In energy terms, or in shillings and pence
Unless you are drilling
And making a killing
Your pockets a-filling - it doesn't make sense >

Change, change, what about change?
Effect on the climate and temperature range
No good to be crying
And wondering whying
When everyone's frying - so what about change

Shale, shale, it's all about shale
Splitting the rock beneath village and vale
Disturbing foundations
With violent vibrations
In ancient locations - it's all about shale

Gas, gas, oh what a gas!
I'm laughing so hard that I fell on my ass
It's all about money
So sad that it's funny
You're taking the piss, honey, oh what a gas

Frack, frack, let's have a frack!
Fuck off you frackers, we all know the crack
Shoot shit down a hollow
Fuck knows what will follow
Go fucking right off and don't fucking come back!

*(Go fucking right off and don't fucking come
back!)*

Demeter And The Poet

'He's taken her away!' The woman cried
He sighed, and put aside his poetry
And sat beneath the tree, and she beside
And listened to her grief. 'Persephone
Has gone to Hades!' How the woman wept
'He took her last year, didn't he?' he said
'Here, have a handkerchief' he said - she kept
On weeping - 'Look, it's not as if she's dead
She's only sleeping.' 'It's alright for you'
She said, 'you're just a poet. You can write
About how black the berries are, how blue
The sloes, how hazel brown and apple bright
And beautiful it is.' 'You don't look bad
Yourself' he said. That poet - what a lad.

Old Women Are The Mistress Of The Lust
That Used To Master Us (That Boy)

'Old women, in the autumn of our lives
may wear the smoke of fires in our hair
be mothers, spinsters, prostitutes or wives
and still have merry ribbons from the fair
sewn on our skirts, and in our corsets laced
and all around our hats, and stockings on
We may be old, and not so sweetly graced
by beauty now our summer days are gone
but autumn still has leaves upon her dress
and berries from her lips to spill, it's just -
(although we have our secrets to confess)
Old women are the mistress of the lust
That used to master us.' 'Oh aye, you try'
That boy - his eyes are bluer than the sky

The Old Man And The Hill

The old man sat and looked up at the hill
I think my work on earth, he said, is done
My finest hour is over. It's been fun
I've lived my life according to my will
And felt the thrill of love and had my fill
My little seeds are growing in the sun
No need for racing now the race is won
No need for ink or paper or a quill

I've written my last lines of poetry
He said, to no-one other than the skies
A sonnet so it was, a eulogy
Remember me (a poet never dies)
The sun grew dim behind the hill and he
Fell silent as the stars began to rise

PROSE

*

Crap Rabbit

Crap Rabbit stuck her nose out of her burrow and
sniffed the air.
Cabbage and poo again.
Crap Rabbit sighed.
Crap Rabbit did a lot of sighing.
Crap Rabbit wrote a lot of things in which other
people sighed as well, and used a lot of words that
rhymed with sighing.
And a lot of 'ings' and 'I's.
And lots of words that rhyme with sky.
And, of late, far too much soppy shit.
Crap Rabbit sighed again.
'Wassup, Crap Rabbit?' asked one of the clouds.
There were a few of them hanging around.
All grey they were, and ever so dull.
One of them hoiked up a greenie.
'Ew' said Crap Rabbit.
'Why the long face?' said the cloud.
Crap Rabbit sighed.
'I'm a rabbit. We just come out this way.'
A beetle beetled past the burrow.
'Wotcha, Crap Rabbit!' it said, cheerily.
'Yo' said Crap Rabbit, 'where are you off to?'
'I'm off to do something moderately useful, and
then maybe some fun stuff' said the beetle, 'wanna
come?'
'Nah' said Crap Rabbit, 'I've got things to do.'
'Like what?'
'Like Really Important Poetry' said Crap Rabbit.
'What, that stuff you write with all the 'I's and
'ings' and things that rhyme with sky, and all the
soppy shit?'
'Yeah, that's right. It's all Really Important.'
One of the clouds sniggered.

'Is it, though?' said the beetle.
Another cloud hoiked up a greenie.
Crap Rabbit looked into the distance.
Crap Rabbit did that a lot.
Crap Rabbit wrote a lot of things in which other
people looked into the distance as well.
Crap Rabbit watched as the cheerful beetle
beetled away into the distance.

See?

Crap Rabbit sighed.

Avebury, April 8th, 2017

Today, after spending a very enjoyable afternoon
taking seven hundred photographs of impossibly
lovely things, I went to Avebury to contemplate
the possible destruction of the known universe.
There, in the circle, a little way away and basking
topless in the spectacular afternoon light, is a
gentleman who appears to be in a similarly
contemplative mood. I think it best to introduce
myself, seeing as how today, like any other day
really, could quite conceivably be our last on
earth.
"Are you Someone Else?" he says.
Somewhere, and I know this to be true, there is
actually someone called 'Gail Someone Else'.
But it's not me.
"No," says I, "I am Gail from Devizes."
He is Graham from Slough.
And he and I agree, surprisingly cheerfully in fact,
that following the US strikes on Syria, we are
most probably all fucked.
And that we have come to Avebury to have a little
think about stuff.
After a short but most pleasant interaction, in the
spirit of universal brotherhood, we shake hands
and have a hug.
And he goes back to basking.
And I get on me bus.
And the birds fly.
And the stones are still the stones.
And all is well.
Avebury stuff, innit.

The Monster up Victoria Road

I'd been meaning to take a photograph of the
Monster up Victoria Road for some time. I got it
together today. Pointed my camera at the tarmac,
took about three, and strolled away.
'Excuse me!' A little red-faced man appeared
behind me. He was carrying a coffee cup, and he
looked a bit cross.
What is this, I thought to myself, somewhat
confused and disorientated by the unplanned
social interaction, I don't remember seeing this in
my diary.
'Why are you taking pictures of my house?' said
the man.
Huh?
Is this it?
The bit where I die a ludicrous death?
'Sorry?'
'Mother said that you were taking pictures of our
house.'
'Oh no' I said, 'I was just taking pictures of the
Monster in the road.'
He hesitated. Not quite the answer he had
expected, methinks.
'Sorry?' he said.
'The Monster in the road' I said, pointing at the
road and then at my camera, 'come and look.'
I showed him the pictures, which were just of the
tarmac, and the Monster in the road.
No other pictures in the camera. None at all.
He looked a bit confused.
He'd have to tell mother about the Monster.
I wonder how that went.
'Oh' he said.
'See?' said I. 'No pictures of your house.'

'It's just that mother said...' he said.
'No, sorry' said I, cheerily.
And strolled away.

2 December 2017

It is sometimes to the poets in our lives that we look for perspective, solace, and inspiration, in these our angst-ridden, dosh-driven, god-forbidden (huh?), petty-stressed existences.

Good luck with that.

Today I meet Andy Fawthrop, formerly known as 'Barred of Bromham' before he came in from the cold and the vegetable fields, by Poundland.

I look to him for answers.

He senses my desperation. It is, after all, barely clothed. If I were to be in fancy dress there would be a tutu involved and I would be carrying like a scroll and an urn or something, and doing a lot of weeping.

Andy understands, and knows just the right words to sort me out good and proper.

'Get over yerself' he says, pithily.

Fucker

Dog Shit 19122017

I'm in the Library And Community Hub.
I smell dog shit.
I look at my hand.
It is covered in dog shit.
The bottom of my bag is also covered in dog shit.
It's a worry.
I sidle to the toilets.
Half the library's supply of tissues and hand soap
go on attempting to clean off the dog shit.
It goes everywhere.
I persist bravely.
I don't even cry.
I am a fighter.
It takes more than being Absolutely Covered In
Dog Shit to get me down.
Twenty minutes later I sidle out of the toilets,
smelling of cheap soap and dog shit.
I smile at the nice ladies at the counter.
They smile back.
As I leave, one of them sniffs the air.
Happy Christmas.

Santa's Trousers

"Do you want me to iron your special Santa trousers for Sunday night, dear?" said Mrs Santa, from the kitchen.
"No" said Santa, "I thought I'd just go out in my underpants this year."
Mrs Santa appeared in the kitchen doorway.
"Not really, dear, surely?"
Santa sighed.
"No, dear, not really."
Mrs Santa laughed.
"Oh, you are a bell end, Mr Santa."

The Angel of the 33

The forecasts vary. Blizzards hitting at 3pm, or
6pm. It's snowing quite a bit in Devizes already,
and it's only 8am. I reckon I'm going to get stuck
in Chippenham. I actually consider not going to
work. I ring my boss. She tells me to stay at
home if I'm worried. I could if I wanted to.
For fuck's sake.
Since when was more concerned about my own
survival than that of others? I think to myself.
And go to work.
I ring the bus company before I go.
Normal service till further notice.
All the cooks, volunteers, and staff have turned
up. Yay.
We look after homeless and vulnerably housed
people.
That's what we do all year.
And that's what we're doing today.
We feed them, give them gloves and stuff, check
that they all have somewhere to stay tonight.
Wiltshire Council have made extra provision for
rough sleepers under the Severe Weather
Emergency Protocol, and some of the churches
are opening their doors over Christmas.
We check that everyone has heating and send
someone up to the Council for a Local Welfare
Provision Payment. New people turn up. We
have a banging lunch. We deal with a small
challenge or two. We do some good work.
Then we put up a notice on the door signposting
rough sleepers to the Council, bypass the usual
debrief, and pack up early.

I get four offers of a lift home, and two offers of a place to stay in Chippenham if the bus doesn't show.

I ring up the bus company.

Normal service till further notice.

The streets have gone quiet. Cars are driving really slowly. The snow is whippy and spiteful in the wind. It's bloody cold.

I wait on my own at the bus stop for the 4pm bus.

I hope it turns up.

Remember the Todesmärsche, I think to myself (as I always do when the weather is bad).

I only have to get to Devizes.

I have boots, and a coat, and only myself to worry about.

For fuck's sake, get a grip.

The bus turns up on time. It's not one of the usual drivers. She's smiling as she pulls into the bus stop.

I fumble in my bag.

'You've got a ticket, then?' she says. 'Yeah, somewhere' says I. 'Oh never mind,' she says, 'just hop on and get warm.'

Four passengers. Old couple. Girl in woolly hat. Me. Windows splattered with mud. Snow falling. Grit on the road.

She's not fussed. 'Let's get back to sunny Devizes, then!' she says, chirpily.

I start to cry. Like a massive wuss. I'm so fucking relieved to be on the bus.

I text my boss to say that I am on the bus and crying like a massive wuss. My boss texts me back. Aw.

At least she won't have to club anyone over the head and nick their 4 by 4 to get me home now. Phew.

I cry a bit more, and the bus trundles on.

Bleak fields. Ancient and terrible silhouettes of trees, stark against the white and sky. Flocks of rooks in the ruts, black on the cold brown earth. And snow.

There's no-one at the bus stop in Calne. There's no-one anywhere, really. A car or two. A few Dads with kids on sleighs. The odd dog-walker. Between Chippenham and Devizes the landscape and the quality of snow changes. Storm Whatever is kicking in. The gritters have been out, but the snow is starting to swirl, and drift, and parts of the road surface look really slippy.

She drives assertively, and only bumps into the pavement twice. 'Ooops, getting a bit slidey there' she says, cheerfully.

One of the other passengers congratulates her. She's doing pretty well, he says. Yeah, I'd agree with that. It's actually a smoother ride than usual. She doesn't suffer tentative drivers gladly, though. 'Oh come on, for God's sake!' 'What on earth are you doing?' 'Get on with it!'.

She's got attitude, alright.

But she isn't rude.

She's hard. She's funny. She can drive a fucking bus.

And she's getting me home.

When we get to Rowde there's a white Council van parked across the road that leads to Dunkirk Hill. She stops the bus and asks why we can't go that way.

According to the man from the Council, Dunkirk Hill is unpassable.

At this point I have the sense that this was my last chance to get back to Devizes.

She argues the toss with the Council man.

'This bus is so bloody slow it'll get up any hill!' she says.
Nope. No way.
She's not happy.
'I suppose if you've blocked the road I can't go that way then' she says (she's exercising some restraint, I feel), and heads for Caen Hill.
Caen Hill is a fast road.
It's not fast now.
Slowly, oh so slowly, ever so slowly, everyone who made it to work, is making for home.
Nearly there.
Past the icy canal by the Black Horse.
Past stuff stuck by Shane's Castle, and some blue lights.
And we're in town.
She stops the bus for me to get off.
'Thank you so much for getting me home' I say, touching her arm, and giving her a ridiculously intense teary look.
'Oh that's alright, love,' she says, with an enormous smile, 'that's my job!'
'Get home safely yourself' I say.

And off she goes.
Into the snow.

Ann and Jack

There are two small girls in my life. One is my god-daughter, Emily, and the other is ('What name would you like to be called if you had another name?') 'Jack'.

It was Jack's birthday yesterday. Candlemas baby. Aw. Yesterday she was eight, and today I have decided that what she needs in her life is a mouth organ. All kids should have a mouth organ. And Lego, and a bike, and love, but Jack's got those already.

It's drizzling as I leave the house. I try not to stop on the bridge but something catches my eye. A kingfisher. Flying in a dead straight line, faster than light and brighter than blue, low above the centre of the canal, under the bridge like an arrow and up, to perch on the branch of a tree.

Kingfishers! Bucket list stuff!

Too rainy for photographs. Damn.

I stand and watch it for a while.

'Hello!' says Lesley.

Lesley is dressed for the weather, and her jolly face is peeping out of something practical.

I've known Lesley a long time. She's always nice to me. I like that.

We chat a bit. Kingfisher. Family. My book. The fringe (not quite sure how we got on to that one).

'What's wrong with it?' says Lesley, concentrating quite hard on my face.

'Well, I've got quite a severe face, and some haircuts soften it and this one doesn't' says I.

She concentrates a bit more.

'OK' she says, 'there is a bit of Ann Widdecombe about it.'

Oh God.

Time stops.

That's like being Michael Howard with a 'bit of the night' about him.

Ann fucking Widdecombe?

All is lost.

Process.

Vanity of vanities, all is vanity.

Process.

Ann fucking Widdecombe?

'For fuck's sake get over yourself' says Andy Fawthrop (who, for the purposes of this piece, has appeared on my shoulder as a slightly sinister mystical parrot).

I express to Lesley that I wish our conversation had ended a little sooner, but that there are no hard feelings.

'You know I'll write about that' says I.

'Oh yes' she says, 'I know you will.'

We part company cheerfully.

Sort of.

It's alright for Lesley.

She doesn't look like Ann Widdecombe.

'Do I look like Ann Widdecombe?' I ask the blokes in the music shop.

Silence. One of them is looking at his computer, and the other looks mildly puzzled but potentially compliant.

'You have to say 'No, Gail, you don't look like Ann Widdecombe" says I.

I raise my hands as if to summon elemental forces. 'One, two, three...!'

'You don't look like Ann Widdecombe' says the mildly puzzled one, politely. The other one is still looking at his computer.

'And you!' says I. He looks up. 'What, sorry?'

'You have to say 'No, Gail, you don't look like Ann
Widdecombe'. Go on!'
'You don't look like Ann Widdecombe' he says,
and goes back to his computer.
'Thanks.'

Armed with a mouth organ (my mate Steve calls it
a gob-iron) in the key of C, I hurtle down the
canal on my bike, gathering spatters of mud on
my clothes and scowling crossly.
I wonder if she means the early Ann, or the new
improved shiny Celebrity Ann?
The year before last I was mistaken for the Rt Hon
Claire Perry, Conservative MP for Devizes.
At least she's...younger.

'She's in her room' says Jack's Mum.
Jack is on her bed, and appears to have grown at
least a foot since Christmas. She's never been a
small child. She's chunky, and energetic, and she
beat all the boys at dodgeball this week. There are
certain games for which you would want Jack on
your side. Like rugby, for instance.
I love Jack.
She rocks.
She's lolling on her tummy with her feet in the air,
in Saturday morning kid mode, dressed in little
black jimmies with the words 'Shine Bright'
written on them.
She's happy to see me. I like that.
'Shut your eyes and open your hands' I say. She
sits up enthusiastically and shuts her eyes.
The little grey box doesn't look very interesting.
She tries to open it but it's a bit fiddly. We help
her. She takes the mouth organ out of the box
carefully and looks at it.

'Blow, then' we say, 'blow in the holes!'
Jack blows.
Oh!
Her face lights up.
Her eyebrows leap a little.
She looks at the mouth organ.
She looks at us.
She looks back at the mouth organ.
She smiles.
'Go on, do it again! Blow and suck and see what
happens!'
She does.
She's amazed.
She blows again.
More amazement.
She's really pleased.
'I wanted one of these!' she says, excitedly, and
blows again.
Then she puts the mouth organ down in her lap,
and looks at her Mum with shiny eyes.
'Do you know' she says.
'I wished for that.'

As I go down the stairs to my bike I can hear Jack
playing the mouth organ.
I'm not really bothered about the whole Ann
Widdecombe thing now.
Who gives a fuck.

Swastika

The windows of the bus are misted up this
morning and, next to a picture of a stick man with
an unfeasibly large member, some kiddy has
drawn a swastika.
As the bus chugs on I contemplate removing the
swastika, and 'how it might look' if I were to up
and walk to the front of the bus and wipe it off.
I actually think about that for twenty minutes.
Then I come to my senses.
If I can't wipe a swastika off a bus window in front
of a bunch of teenagers how will the war ever be
won.
All those poor people who died.
All those brave people who protested and died.
All those good people who fought and died.
And I am thinking twice about it?
Pathetic.
I get up and walk to the front of the bus and wipe
the swastika off with the words "I'm sorry (wtf?),
but I can't sit looking at a swastika all the way to
Chippenham".
The kiddy laughs.
I sit down.
The bus chugs on.

Mohammed

'So, what's the most popular tourist attraction at
the moment?' I ask Mohammed the 4.7 star Uber
driver, as we crawl through Hyde Park at a snail's
pace in the dark and the rain.
'Here,' says Mohammed, gesturing at the traffic,
'this. People like to buy expensive cars and drive
through Central London really slowly to show
them off.'
I look out of the window. He's not wrong. There
are some very ostentatious vehicles glinting under
the street lamps.
Rain on new money. Shiny.
'And shisha cafes' says Mohammed. 'Shisha cafes
are springing up everywhere. Shisha cafes on the
Edgeware Road.'
'And what are people talking about?' I ask (always
an interesting question to ask taxi drivers and
hairdressers).
'Money' says Mohammed. 'How to make lots of
money quickly.'
Then he tells me that since the Arab Spring more
and more people want to come and live in London
because their money is safer here than in other
countries where there is war and corruption.
'What's the worst thing that can happen to their
money here?' he says, shrugging.
I look out of the window at the ostentatious cars
cruising through the dark of Hyde Park, and see
something I haven't seen before.
London through Mohammed's eyes.
And rain on new money.
Shining.

Scandalous Dance Moves

Steve Doolan has come up with one of his wanky
word challenges again. The last time he did this
the word was 'equidistant', which I managed to
drop in to a conversation at the doctor's whilst
being injected for reasons that now elude me.
This time it is the phrase 'scandalous dance
moves'.
I'm going to the dentist today.
Perfect.

In the dentist's waiting room two jolly identically
bearded gentlemen are indulging in witty
repartee. I smile at them in an attempt to
establish a bond that will allow me to insert the
phrase without being inappropriately intrusive.
They smile back. I smile again. Moments come,
moments go, openings present themselves,
openings close before I can get a word in
edgeways, we all smile a bit more, and then
they're gone.

'Mrs Foster?' says the dentist. I hate that.
Usually I would say, somewhat chippily, 'It's Ms,
actually', but today I can't be arsed.
I inform her that I am likely to burst in to tears for
no apparent reason.
'Is it me?' she says.
She's nice. She looks concerned.
I reassure her that it is symptomatic of my usual
volatile mental state rather than being indicative
of fear, and that, as she is not wearing a blood-
stained apron and wielding a rusty pair of pliers,
I'm not really bothered.

I stare obediently into the blinding light above the chair, and open my mouth.

She does her dentist thing. It's warm in the chair and nothing hurts at all. I drift off while she chats to her equally nice assistant about how cold it is outside and what they are doing at the weekend. Then she mentions skirts. Then she mentions making lots of glittery skirts. Then she mentions people running. Then she mentions lots of people running in the glittery skirts she is making.

'Arggh' says I.
I know a fucking moment when it comes along. 'Arggh'.
She pulls her dental thingy out of my mouth.
'Will you be busting any scandalous dance moves in your glittery skirts?' says I.

BOOM BOOM TSHHH

'No' says the dentist, deadpan, 'we're running a marathon for my friend's son. He's got cancer and he won't live past January. We're raising money for Clic Sergeant, and to help him tick things off his bucket list. He's ticked off quite a few things already.'

Right. That isn't funny at all.
I feel a bit bad.

'Look, I'll show you the skirts' she says, and shows me her phone, and pictures of her mates running along with her cute little glittery ra-ra skirts over their leggings.
I feel so bad that I am moved to tell her about the 'scandalous dance moves' thing.

There is a short silence. She and her assistant
laugh politely. I don't think they really get it but
they don't seem to mind. They've had far odder
things happen during the course of the dental day
than the Steve Doolan Scandalous Dance Moves
Challenge.

Worse things happen at sea.

I ask her about the little lad. He's taking it very
well, apparently, and all of his mates have been
wonderful.

He's thirteen.

It's all a bit fucking poignant.
I don't know what to say.
I give her a pathetic donation, and say how sorry I
am, and thank you, and goodbye.

'You didn't cry' she says, as I go out the door.
'No', says I, somewhat surprised.
I didn't.

The Depression Fairy

She's here again.
Sitting in the corner in an old grey dress, weeping.
She looks like me.
Older, though, more haggard.
Face like a wet weekend.
No time for anyone but herself.
I like her not.
It's not like I invited her.
She just appears.
Year after year.
'Would you like a tissue?' I ask her.
Her nose is running and the snot is mingling with
her tears.
She really should change that dress.
'No' she says, looking out of the window,
mournfully, and then, as an afterthought, 'thank
you.'
'Would you like a cup of tea?'
'No, thank you.'
Sniff.
She won't eat anything, but the biscuits keep
disappearing.
She smokes, she coughs, she cries, she smokes
some more, she coughs again, she plays with her
hair.
Hair that could do with a wash.
Sometimes I switch the television on for her.
She'll watch for a while.
About five minutes, usually.
Then her gaze will drift back to the window.
There's no amusing her, however hard I try.
She doesn't want to do anything but cry, and feel
sorry for herself.
She's really annoying.

I've suggested it all to her. Light boxes, Vitamin D, regular walks, sleep, food, CBT, spiritual practice, visit to the doctor, anti-depressants, even the nuclear 'Get over yourself' option.
She's too far gone for any of it.
She's drowning.
'No' she says, with a martyred air, 'all I need is Spring.'
Sniff.
Like I can give her that.
'Maybe you should spend more time with friends and family,' I suggest (thinking that will be fun for them), 'or do something for someone else to take you out of yourself. Or think how bad some people have it. Or something.'
She flickers a bit.
In January she was quite a solid sort of grey.
It's February now, and I can see through her.
Fingers crossed she'll be gone soon.
I hope it's early in March, like last year, rather than later like the year before.
She's really fucking annoying.
'You know you can talk to me.' I say.
'Yes,' she says, 'thanks.'
Silence.
Martyred look.
Window.
Tears.
Nothing to be done then, I guess.
Except to make myself a cup of tea.
And wait for Spring.
And watch her drown.

'Are we nearly there yet?'
'Nearly.'

Sniff.
Not fucking nearly enough.

Job Done

It began when the nights grew dark. Quiet at first, like a feeble fingernail, scratching, and then a scurrying, as faint as mice with feather dusters on their feet.

'That's just the wind' she thought. 'That's just the old building, creaking.'

And she would lie there awake awhile, listening. And her eyes would droop and her limbs grow heavy and...there it was again...the scurrying.

One night she got up and looked in the cupboards. 'What am I doing?' she thought, and went back to bed.

Scurry, scurry, shuffle and scratch.

One night there was a bang. It came from the dustiest cupboard of all, the one in the spare room with the Memories in. She didn't like that cupboard. Never opened it. If she opened it the Memories would fall out, and she would have to look at them.

So she hid under the duvet and wished for morning.

Scurry, shuffle, scratch, and bang.

Tiny footprints on the bookshelf. Well, boot prints, really. And a book fallen out of the shelf. And odd little swishing marks across the dusty mirror in the hallway.

Nah.

She picked up the book. It belonged in the Memories cupboard really, with all the other shit, but it was useful. She put it back on the shelf.

The voice started in late January. It seemed to be coming from the cupboard, but not always. It would wait for her to fall asleep before it started. It sounded like an angry mosquito, but there were words in there somewhere. They weren't very nice words, and they sounded awfully familiar. There was more scurrying, and the bangs became more frequent, and seemed to come from everywhere.

She started to feel a little unwell. The voice kept waking her up and saying nasty things in her ear. The house was dark and dirty, and it was too cold to have the windows open.

Then it started in the daytime. The scurrying, the scratching, the bangs. She looked in all the cupboards, under the bed, in the drawers, behind the cooker. Nothing. Only tiny bootprints in the grime and dust, and the whiny voice in her ear, day in, day out. She could make out the words now. 'Pathetic', 'Look at you!' 'Look at the state of it'.

She began to despair.

One night she got the rounders bat and threw all the cupboards open and stood in the middle of the living room half naked, and shouted 'Come here and face me like a man!'

Nothing. Just a faint snigger and a scratch. In the morning the book was on the floor again, and the word 'Pathetic' was written in a faint scratch in the dust of the bookshelf.

She still hadn't opened the Memory cupboard.

Then one day the sun shone, and she had a very
strange thought.
Maybe I should do some cleaning.
It was such a strange thought that she didn't
really know what to do with it.
She got a kitchen wipe, and wiped the bootprints
off the top of the bookshelf, and sat down, and
had a think.
Hmm. That felt good.
The next day she threw something away.
And the next.
And the next.
Then she got the hoover out.
And the mop.
It was all very exciting.

The more she cleaned, the louder the scurrying,
the more she dusted, the louder the scratch. At
night the bangs were terrifying, but every day she
got up and threw something away, and slowly,
ever so slowly, the house got cleaner.

She opened the curtains. She opened the
windows. She washed the windows with
newspaper and vinegar like Granny used to do.
She polished the crystals and dusted the picture
frames, threw out the out-of-date cup-a-soups
and medicines, made lots of trips to the bins, and
carried on cleaning.

Until all that was left was the Memory cupboard.

It was a Monday at noon, and the cupboard stood
by the window in the bedroom emitting a small
hiss. She approached it assertively, armed with a

black plastic sack for rubbish, shoebox for things to keep, tweezers, a torch, and a rounders bat.

As she opened the door, things fell out. A book, some train tickets, photographs, postcards, some drawings, an old watch, a badly carved piece of wood, a sailor's hat and an old packet of tobacco, all spilled out on the floor at her feet, in a cloud of dust.

There were still more things in the cupboard, and something scratching and hissing behind them. She rummaged through the things on the floor. It was all crap really. Crap with no emotion attached to it. Not any more.

Why have I kept these things? she thought, as she picked up the sailor's hat and put it in the black plastic sack. Then the book, and the train tickets, and everything else, till the things on the floor were all sorted and there were only the depths of the cupboard to plumb.

One thing at a time, went into the sack. Nothing went into the shoebox, nothing at all.

The cupboard was nearly empty now.
Hiss. Scratch. Spit.
Last bit of crap in the black plastic sack, and...

There he was.
In the corner of the cupboard.
Now all the crap had gone he had nowhere to hide.

He pressed himself into the corner of the
cupboard, and spat, and bared his teeth at her,
and waved his tiny fist.
He was all of three inches high.
'You look so tiny in the cupboard!' she said,
laughing.
'You're pathetic!' he squeaked.
He looked very red, and miniscule beads of sweat
were forming on his miniature monobrow.
She laughed again.
In broad daylight she could see him for what he
really was.
A really tiny little man.

'You going to go easy or do I have to use the
rounders bat?' she said.
He cowered in the corner of the cupboard.
'Don't hurt me!'

Tweezers, then. She picked him up carefully. She
tried not to hurt him. He was, after all, so very
tiny, and he looked kind of sad hanging from the
tweezers by the label of his tiny jumper. He
hissed, and spat again.

'Out to the bins with you, my lad!' she said, and
marched down the stairs to the bin store, and
threw him in the bin, where he landed on top of
some old cabbage scrapings and a nappy.

He looked up at her with mournful eyes.
'I guess that's it, then' he said.

'Oh yes' she said, and slammed down the bin lid.

Back upstairs she watched out of the vinegar and newspaper shiny windows as the bin men came, and waved as the bin he was in was emptied into the back of the cart. Then she watched as the lorry drove away, turned away from the window, went into the living room, and listened.

Silence.
Just silence.
And a single shaft of light, shining on the bookshelf.

She dusted off her hands, and sat down.

Job done.

Stories

I went to see my elderly friend Gloria today.
Gloria has memory issues, and suffers from a lack
of conversation, but she's no less witty and
twinkly-eyed than she was the last time I visited.
We sing 'All Things Bright And Beautiful'
together, and I read my 'Emily's Books' story to
her.
'Emily's Books' is about the day I read stories with
my god-daughter and her Mum, and one of the
last lines is 'It's a long time since someone read
me a story.'
There's a kind of awesome perfection in reading
'Emily's Books' to Gloria, because it's a long time
since anyone read her a story too.
"I live in books" she says, smiling.
There are three books on a small shelf next to her
chair.
One is a copy of Jilly Cooper's 'Appassionata'.
I confess to some surprise.
"Isn't that a bit...raunchy, Gloria?"
"Oh, I don't mind that" she says, "it's all part of
life."
And then she looks at me with a serious face and
says...

"What I see when I look at you is stories.
And the unknown."

Michael

I first met, let's call him 'Michael', in 2014, on a
Sunday morning at about half past seven, by the
graveyard on my way to church.
Michael always has tears in his eyes.
He was visiting his wife in the graveyard.
At that point in time he was visiting her twice a
day.
She passed away in 2009.
Five years is a long time to cry.

There was a time when I met Michael less.
He had cancer.
His son died.
I bump into him The Brittox these days. usually
by Boots.
He's 86 and still alive.
Something to do with the twinkle that shines
behind his tears, perhaps.
That and his friends.
The ones that are still alive, that is.

Yesterday, I went out to take photographs.
Sometimes when I do this, I go where the wind
takes me. It seemed to be taking me down to the
fields, when I noticed a tree in the graveyard, lit
by a shaft of autumn sun, with many coloured
leaves around its feet.

I didn't really want to go into the graveyard. Bit
morbid and that. The skies are dark enough
without dwelling too much on death. But hey,
follow the wind...

I fannied about taking photos of trees and stone
angels for a while, and then decided to go to the
new part of the graveyard, where there is a good
view of Roundway Hill.

At the far end of the graveyard was a man stood
alone by a gravestone, with his head bowed.
That looks like Michael, I thought to myself.
And it was.

"So this is (let's call her 'Jane') your wife" I say.
"Yes" says Michael, "and my son is over there."
He points to another headstone, a little way away.
His eyes are full of tears.
Eight years is a long time to cry.

Michael is pleased to see me, and I'm kind of
pleased to meet Jane after all this time.

She has a black shiny headstone, with words and
flowers engraved upon it, and there are artificial
flowers in vases on her grave.

I ask about Jane's neighbour. Michael knew him,
and most of the other people buried in the vicinity
of his wife's grave.
When the time comes, he will be buried there too.
We agree that it is lovely in the graveyard, in sight
of the hill, and that it is a good place to be.

He asks me how I am.
I think twice about mentioning my book.
I've been carrying a copy round with me to show
people but it's hardly the time for marketing.

But it really does seem like a moment for poetry.
I think once. I think twice. I decide.

"Can I read you something?" I say.
"Of course you can" says Michael.

So there, by Jane's grave, I read him 'Waiting For
You; The Return of the Light'.

There is silence for a moment.
Michael is not the only one with eyes full of tears.
Forever is a long time to cry.

And then he says...
"That's beautiful."

And it was.

Renee

My Granny was mad. And her mother before her,
I think. My Granny's name was Irene. She was my
Mum's Mum. Mad Renee, my Dad called her.

Renee lived in a world of her own, and believed in
fairies. She ate lettuce, and Shreddies with honey,
like a little bird. She was an innocent, and would
have kept us all innocent forever. There was no
pain in Renee's world. I wasn't allowed to see
Robert Powell die on the cross. It was 'All Things
Bright And Beautiful', or nothing. Roses in the
garden, songs round the piano, fairy cakes, Peter
Rabbit, and let's pretend.

At night, when she tucked me and my sister in,
she would sing 'Edelweiss' to us, and put kisses in
our hands for us to put under our pillows.
I saw her without her teeth in one night. She was
terrifying. When Renee was old, her tenuous grip
on reality slipped completely, and she would run
outside in her nightie, screaming.

I loved Renee, and my Gramps. The days of my
childhood that I spent at my grandparents' house
were some of the happiest of my life, and the
images of the only place that ever stayed the same
in my life are burned in my brain forever.
Gramps's shed, the attic, the vegetable patch, the
secret door to the Rec, the tiny pond, the fish, the
little statue of Mary Ellen dipping her toe in the
water, the birds, the flowers, the pantry, the
cabinets full of tiny ornaments, the toys that Mum
played with as a child; all so sweet, all so lavender
fragranced and lovely.

And gone.
All gone.

The most powerful memory I have of Renee is
when she took me to see the Cambridge orchestra,
in which my Gramps was playing the electric
guitar.
I must have been about seven at the time. Seven is
the age at which you start to understand the
mysteries of life and death.
Renee wore a fur that night, but I'm going to let
her off.
As we were waiting for the orchestra to begin, our
hands were rested side by side on the arm of the
seat.
I looked at her hand next to mine, and saw how
very different it was.
The skin on her tiny bird fingers was blue veined,
and paper thin, and old, oh so very old.
I looked at my child's hand, all chubby, and pink,
and warm, and young.
I looked back at Renee's hand.
I looked at our hands together.
And I understood something.
My hand will look as old as Renee's hand one day,
I thought to myself.
And the orchestra started to play.

Winkles

I went to see Gloria yesterday.
It took her a lot longer to walk across the room
and search through her mental cupboards than it
did the last time I saw her.
'I like to think before I speak' she said.
So she'd think.
Then she'd start a sentence, and not be able to
finish it.
Then she'd start the sentence again and get a little
further this time.
And then not be able to finish it.
Again.
And again.
And again.
And then she'd give up.
I fear that there is less in Gloria's mental
cupboards than there was before.
She was exasperated.
'I'm so stupid' she said.
No she isn't.
'You just need more stimulation' I said.
'Oh I don't stimulate myself, dear' she said.
She knew what she was saying.
'How very racy of you, Gloria!'
Oh how we laughed.
The rest of our time together was taken up with
me looking for things she had lost, and singing.
Gloria knows every word of 'Lord of the Dance',
and more verses than I do of 'There Is A Green
Hill Far Away.'
And I read her a bit of my poetry. She liked that.
It's not like she could get away.
After I over-acted 'Mischievous Spring' for her, we
somehow got on to the subject of ditzyness, which

is one of my least favourite and most annoying qualities.

'Chase me, I'm full of winkles!' said Gloria, with a little wriggle, and a twinkle in her eye.
'That's what my mother used to say.'

Gloria is 87.

Noel Fielding

'What's that you're cooking, Gail?'
Why is Noel Fielding in the kitchen?
'Well tonight, Noel, I am cooking porridge, with a
scabby apple, and a couple of sugar cubes, in a
water sauce.'
Noel's eyes glaze over.
'Banging', he says, and wafts away.
Wanker.

Toast

'What's that you're cooking, Gail?'
Damn. It's Noel Fielding again. I really must
remember to lock the door in future.
'Well, Noel, tonight I am mostly cooking a bar of
Galaxy between two pieces of buttered wholemeal
toast.'
'Cosmic', says Noel, brushing a soft strand of hair
out of his eyes and doing a little pirouette.
'It's just fucking toast, Noel.'

Paul Hollywood

'What's that you're cooking, Gail?'
That doesn't sound like Noel...
A cold shiver runs down my spine.
Really must put some glass in those windows.
I turn.
Oh God.
It's Paul Hollywood.
Nah.
That's quite enough of that game.

Marbles

'I see you've brought your camera again' said the psychiatrist.
'How very observant of you' she said.
'I wonder if you hide behind it at times.'
She looked down at the camera.
It was a big camera, but she was a lot bigger.
'People can still see me' she said.
'And how does that make you Feel?'
'Visible.'
His pocket tinkled.
'Excuse me' he said, getting up from his chair and standing near the window.
'Yes, snugglebunny, chicken nuggets would be lovely. Yes, love you too, yes more than I loved you yesterday, yes, have you taken your tablets? Well done. Love you, yes, love you.'
He sat down.
'Sorry about that' he said.
'I'm curious to know why you have a Tinkerbell ringtone' she said.
He flushed slightly and rustled his papers.
'It's not about me, we're here to talk about you.'
She looked out of the window.
The clock ticked.
Three texts arrived in his pocket.
He checked his watch.
'I think we should try something different today' he said.
He opened a desk drawer and took out a box, and placed it in front of her.
She looked at the box.
Last week he had given her a doll to play with.
It hadn't gone well.
'Open it' he said.

She opened it.

Fuck! Marbles! All different colours and some plain ones as well! Marbles! All shiny see through and rolly-about and stuff! Oooo!

'I wonder how you Feel about marbles' he said.

She folded her arms, and looked out of the window.

'They're alright.'

'Knowing how much you like photography' he said, 'I thought it would be a good idea for you to take some photographs of the marbles and then afterwards we can talk about them and how they make you Feel.'

For fuck's sake.

Another text arrived in his pocket.

'I'm going to leave the room' he said, 'and when I come back you can show me your photographs.'

The door slammed.

She looked at the marbles.

I know your fucking game, she thought.

And I might just play along.

Click, click...

Chasing the Carriage; a photographer's story
~ *for Amy and Arran and Esmae*

Today I had the privilege of photographing my friend Amy and her husband Arran's wedding blessing. It was lovely seeing people love each other; friends, family, lovers. It was a happy, fun sort of a day, and Amy looked beautiful. I look forward to editing the photographs. There's a bit of a story behind some of them. Here it is:

The blessing is on a farm in Potterne, and Amy has sent me the details of the route that the carriage is taking. I work out that if the horses are walking on the flat and trotting up hills it should be possible for me to photograph the carriage in town, whizz across The Green on my bicycle, get ahead of it, take photographs at specific points along the way, take a sneaky short cut by the fire station in Potterne, and get to the venue first to photograph it arriving.

That's if there is a byway by the fire station. The map says there is but you never know. Even with that it might be cutting it a bit fine. There's a fair few hills on the way to the farm, and too many fags have taken their toll. Be good if it worked though.

I lurk by St James' on the corner and frame a few shots. Get the church tower in, and then maybe The Crammer in the background. It's possible. I photograph a tractor. It's pissing down. I worked out an elaborate way to attach a brolly to my bicycle earlier, so I undo the elaborate attachment, put up the brolly, and practice doing everything with one hand. It's windy. The rain is blowing around and I'm worried about it getting on my camera lens, the umbrella is a massive pain in the ass, and there's lots of traffic.

I wait. Some bloke leans out of his car and informs me that it has stopped raining. It hasn't. A couple of annoying types are coming towards me on the pavement. They'd better not talk to me at this precise moment. If they do I'll have to do that pretending-I-don't-remember-having-met-someone thing I've learned recently. I scowl in a friendly but detached fashion and they walk on by.

And here it comes. A carriage, containing my friend Amy and her baby and family, driven by two very smart carriage persons, and pulled by two beautiful black horses. I position my camera and umbrella and skip about on the side of the road. Yep, good, good, nice view there, click, perfect, and again...

What?

The carriage has turned down a road I didn't expect it to turn down. I run to my bicycle, take a quick shot of the carriage disappearing into the distance across The Crammer, chuck my camera in my basket where it gets rained on, try to do up the complicated umbrella attachment thing, and cross the road. In the middle of the road the umbrella comes loose and gets tangled with my feet. 'Sorry!' I mouth to the traffic, as I untangle myself. Then I'm back on the bike, and back at it, with everything still to play for...

Over The Green, and over The Other Green, and I'm puffed out already. The carriage is way in front, and about to go down the hill out of town.

I like a nice plan to come to fruition. I'm persistent, I'm obstinate, and I have stamina. I chase the carriage. There's quite a lot of traffic behind it, but they're overtaking, and all of a sudden I'm right behind the carriage and, fuck it, I'm going to overtake it as well.

'Wotcha!' I shout, as I whizz past.
'Gail!' squeals Amy.
Brilliant.

Whoosh! And off I go, all the way down to the bottom of the hill out of town, nearly losing control of my bike with the wild exhilaration of it all. I throw the bike in the hedge and wait for the carriage to emerge from the greenery. Clip clop, clip clop, here it comes, click, click, stand in the road in front of the carriage, click, get out of the road quick, carriage going by, click.

Then the long, long, hill into Potterne...

I push my bike slowly. Halfway up the hill I run out of breath. It's not raining any more, the sun is hot. and I'm a middle-aged woman who smokes too much tobacco. I stop, put my hands on my hips, try to breathe, walk a bit, stop, try again, keep walking, stop. I don't reckon I'm going to get that Potterne High Street shot after all, and

the chances of beating the carriage at this point
are slim. Might even miss the service.

A long snake of traffic has accumulated behind
the carriage, and is moving at the same pace that I
am. A kind friend stops and opens her car
window and asks if I want a lift. She looks
concerned, and she's going my way. I decline. Bit
stubborn of me but hey, Plan A, the party isn't
over till whoever sings. And anyway, I'm over the
hill now (in more ways than one).

I get back on my bike, ride as fast as I can, and get
to the church corner in Potterne just in time to get
a long shot of the carriage turning right by the
George and Dragon. I race along the High Street
and turn to follow it up the next hill. It's out of
sight now but I can still hear it clip, clop, clip,
clopping in the distance.

I have to get off the bike again halfway up the hill.
Stop. Breathe. Walk a bit. Stop. Hands on hips.
Breathe. I look at my watch. Hmm. All a bit nail
biting. If there is hope, it lies in the byway...

There it is. The byway by the fire station. A
bridleway, the sign says. Whatever. Looks
bumpy. No path or anything. But there's still a
faint possibility that if I go hell for leather I might
get to the farm before the horses. Bump, rattle,
bump, rattle, clip, clopping in the distance, bump,
rattle. I have visions of coming off the bike, which
is not built for off-roading, banging my head, and
being found by a dog walker two weeks later. The
breathing thing's a bit tricky. Wheeze, rattle,
bump, clip, clop, bump, rattle, wheeze. Are we

nearly there yet? I look at the OS map in my
mind's eye.

Yes.

Ha! The road!
Ha! The farm!
I look around for the carriage.
Nope.
Not here yet.
I take up a position and wait.
Five minutes.
Clip clop, clip clop.
I see the top of the carriage over the hedge in the
distance.
Clip clop, clip clop...

And here it comes. A carriage, containing my
friend Amy and her baby and family, driven by
two very smart carriage persons, and pulled by
two beautiful black horses.

Click, click.

The Vegetable Shop Man

The vegetable shop man and I are looking at the
window of the second-hand shop across the road,
in which someone has been mildly satirical about
the Royal Wedding.
You've got to love a mildly satirical window
dresser.
At least I think they've been satirical.
Cardboard masks of the Royal family grin wonkily
from assorted mannequins dressed in second
hand wedding outfits.
William looks alright, but The Queen looks
minging.
'Posh and Becks' he says, despairingly.
'Fake celebrities' says I.
'They're no more celebrities than we are' he says.
'All a distraction from what's really going on'
says I.
We look at the mannequins again.
He shrugs.
I sigh.
'I don't want to hear about it' he says.
'What about Gaza, and Israel?'
'Indeed' says I.
A short silence ensues, within which develops a
mutual understanding that all we can do about it
is just crack on.
'Bye then' I say.
'Bye' he says.
'Hope you sell a lot of strawberries!'
The vegetable man smiles.

Virgin

The early bus pulls in at the bus stop by the
garage, and two people get off.

She's about twenty five, and is wearing a smart
cotton dress and tidy plaits.
He's about the same age, maybe a bit older, and is
sporting a grubby vest, and tracksuit bottoms over
which his stomach spills.

'Are you going to stay a virgin all your life?' he
says to her.

And off they walk to town, with the warm breeze
blowing between them.

What's Coming Home?

'What's coming home?'
'The World Cup, Mother.'
'What, like in 1966?'
'Yes, Mother.'
'When they said it was all over but it wasn't
really?'
'Yes, Mother.'
'Is that Bobby Moore in the waistcoat? What a
lovely boy.'
'No, Mother, that's Gareth Southgate. He's the
manager.'
'And who are the little lads?'
'They're the players, Mother.'
'And where are the Germans?'
'There aren't any Germans.'
'Bet there are somewhere.'
'Biscuit?'
'Who did you say was coming home again?'
'The World Cup, Mother.'
'What, like in 1966?'

Etc.

Welding

'Aw, look, it's another Royal Wedding.'
'What? Welding? Who's welding?'
'Eugenie.'
'Why is Eugenie welding?'
'Eugenie isn't welding.'
'Why not?'
'It's her wedding.'
'Who's welding?'
'No-one. It's Eugenie's wedding.'
'Shame about the welding.'

'Who's Eugenie?'

Etc

The Invitation

Vladimir's party invitation sat on the mantlepiece
between two framed photographs of himself half-
naked on horses.
It was garishly bright in the gloom.
Vladimir took it down and looked at it.
The invitation was covered with pink balloons and
party whistles and champagne glasses, and
Donald himself had written on it in red crayon.
'Plees come to my party' it said.
'Bring a bottel' it said.
'PS don't be meen or u won't know what hit u' it
said.
Vladimir raised an eyebrow and one corner of his
mouth (but not so much that you'd notice), and
put the invitation back on the mantlepiece
carefully.
He went to his needlework box and, after some
consideration, chose a nice red ribbon.
He went to his desk and selected some cheerful
Communist wrapping paper.
He went and looked under his bed, and pulled out
a big shiny black box.
He carried the box back in to the great hall, and
sat down on his favourite chair and began to
wrap.
When he had finished the present it looked
beautiful.
He put it on a table, poured himself a coffee so
strong you could stand a stick up in it, and stood
and admired it for a while.
'I can't wait to see his face' thought Vladimir.
The ghost of a snigger and the shadow of a smirk
passed over his face, and his shoulders shook
slightly.

'After all, it is almost as good to give as it is to receive'
Vladimir looked in the mirror over the mantlepiece.
He shot himself a sneer.
Or was it a smile.
He winked at himself.
He checked out his profile.
He winked at his profile.
He got a smaller mirror, and checked out how he looked from behind winking at himself.
He smiled again.
Or was it a sneer.
Either way he was still looking good.

And Donald was going to love, just love, those chocolate covered brussel sprouts...

Terribly Tiresome

'I'm just so frightfully bored' she said.

The butler put the silver tray down on the table,
and adjusted the miniature orchid in the tiny vase
next to the fairy cakes.
'May I suggest a little embroidery, ma'am?'
'Embroidery? How dreadfully dull.'
'Or some letter writing, perhaps?'
He poured the Earl Grey from the delicate china
teapot into the delicate china cup without spilling
a drop, and handed it to her.
'Drinking tea' she sighed, crooking her little finger
as she sipped, 'can be awfully tiring.'
He opened the curtains with a swish.
'Must you?' she said, shading her eyes from the
light.
'It is three in the afternoon, ma'am.'
The tea cup was very heavy. She took three sips,
held it up to the light to admire the colour co-
ordination of her lipstick on the rim with the
intricate rosebud pattern on the china, and put it
down on the tray.
'Fairy cake, ma'am?'
'Must I?'
She picked up the fairy cake.
'Truffles and gold dust again?' she sighed.
'I'm afraid so, ma'am.'
A tear welled up in the corner of her eye.
She put down the fairy cake, lay back on the
chaise longue with the back of her hand over her
brow, and gazed out of the window.
'Will that be all, ma'am?' he said, picking up the
tea tray.

She waved him away weakly.
'Yes, that is all.'

'Wait!'
He turned around.
'What's that?' she said, sitting up and pointing
towards the open window.
'What, ma-am?'
'The smoke on the hill and the sound of shouting.'
He walked over to the window.
'Ah, that' he said.
'That, ma-am, is the world burning.'
'Is that all?'
'Indeed' he said.
She lay back on the chaise longue with the back of
her hand over her brow again, and yawned.

'How terribly tiresome.'

Crap Rabbit and the Butterflies

Crap Rabbit sat outside her burrow and grumbled.
'Why ya grumblin', Crap Rabbit?' asked the butterflies.
'Well' said Crap Rabbit, 'it's because...'
'We're listening, really we are!' said the butterflies, as they carried on fluttering from flower to flower.
'...and that's it, really' said Crap Rabbit, thirty minutes later.
One of the butterflies had fallen asleep on a sunflower and was snoring, and had to be nudged awake.
'Oh! Er...poor you, Crap Rabbit!' it said.
'Sounds like you've no-one to blame but yourself on all counts' said the other butterfly, briskly.
'Yeah' said Crap Rabbit, 'thanks for that.'
'You're welcome!' said the butterflies.

And off they fluttered.

THE END

Gail Foster is a poet, writer, and photographer from Devizes in Wiltshire.

She counts among the highlights of her short and somewhat belated writing career the inclusion of seventeen of her syllables in Quarterday, a journal of classical poetry, appearances on local radio and at Open Mic nights, reading her work at the Gorsedd at Avebury, and having one of her poems included in a service in Salisbury Cathedral. She also enjoys writing arts reviews, and is fond of the odd commission.

In the summer Gail can be seen lurking on street corners, smiling enigmatically at pigeons and concentrating on things.

www.gailfromdevizes.com
www.rhymeandlight.com
https://www.facebook.com/gailfromdevizes/

Printed in Great Britain
by Amazon